The Hunt Museum
Essential Guide

THE HUNT MUSEUM
ESSENTIAL GUIDE

S C A L A

Scala Publishers
in association
with the
Hunt Museum

THE
HUNT
MUSEUM

First published in 2002 by Scala Publishers Ltd
4th Floor, Gloucester Mansions,
140a Shaftesbury Avenue, London WC2H 8HD

Distributed outside The Hunt Museum
in the book trade in the USA and Canada by
Antique Collectors' Club Ltd
Market Street Industrial Park,
Wappingers' Falls, NY 12590, USA

ISBN: 1 85759 287 5

All measurements are in centimeters

Edited by Helen Armitage
Designed by James Shurmer
Produced by Scala Publishers Ltd
Printed and bound in Italy

The Hunt Museum Editorial Team:
Peter McNamara
Fiona Davern
Clodagh Lynch
Geroge Stacpoole
John Hunt

Front cover: Nicolas Froment, *God the Father*
(detail), 15th century

Back cover: Midleton Mace, Irish, 18th century

Acknowledgements

The Hunt Museum acknowledges the
financial assistance of an anonymous donor,
without whose help this book could not have
been published. The editorial team acknowledges the assistance given by Naomi O'Nolan
and Nora Hickey

Photographic Credits

Davison and Associates Ltd: all the images in
this book, with the exception of images listed
below

Studioworks: pages 57, 69, 71, 78, 96 and 172

Courtesy of the Hunt family: pages 10–15

Kevin Wallace Photography: pages 16, 17

Copyright Credits

Pablo Picasso © Succession Picasso/DACS,
2002: page 23

Jack B. Yeats © Courtesy of the Artist's
Estate: page 25

Henry Moore © The Henry Moore
Foundation: pages 32 and 36

CONTENTS

List of Contributors   6

Foreword   7
George Stacpoole, *Chairman, The Hunt Museum*

Introduction   9
The Formation of the Collection and Foundation
of the Hunt Museum

List of Patrons   20

A Selection of 150 Works from the Hunt Collection   21

    Painting   23

    Ceramics   38

    Ivory, Bone, Coral and Glass   76

    Metal   94

    Wood, Textiles and Leather   140

    Stone   155

Index   173

LIST OF CONTRIBUTORS

Jonathan Benington 31
Cormac Bourke 98, 104
Mary Cahill 124
Grace Cantillon 30, 79, 102, 114, 143, 165
Shae Clancy 169
Rose Cleary 43
Fionnuala Croke 24, 26
Anne Crookshank 33
Fiona Davern 141, 154
Mairead Dunlevy 46
Desmond Fitzgerald 35
Peter Francis 60–75
Peter Harbison 101, 108, 119
Tony Harpur 27, 38, 111
Christina Haywood 47, 48, 50, 159, 160
Nora Hickey 23, 34, 37, 93
Jim Higgins 40, 76, 105, 122, 151, 153, 162
Pat Humphreys 77, 92
Alan Johnston 150
Carleton Jones 99, 103, 155, 164, 167
Catherine Lawless 28, 29
Clodagh Lynch 112
Michael Lynch 131, 132, 139, 158, 172
Andy McCarthy 140
John McCormack 44, 54, 55, 106, 109, 121, 123

Elizabeth McCrum 81, 117, 120, 138, 149
Clare McCutcheon 56, 57, 58, 59
Sybille McGovern 80
Pat McKenna 53, 127, 129
Peter McNamara 91
Irene Macken 41, 42, 45, 49, 146, 156
Catherine Marshall 32, 36
Mary M. Moore 116
Kathy Moynes 168
Lynda Mulvin 133, 134, 161, 163
Mary O'Connor 144, 145, 147, 148, 171
Raghnall Ó Floinn 135, 136, 137
Elaine O'Malley 78, 82, 83, 84, 87–9, 90
Naomi O'Nolan 51, 52
Nancy Punch 152
Hilary Pyle 25
John Sheehan 100, 113, 118
Andrew Smith 107
Neal Spencer 110, 157, 166
George Stacpoole 39
Roger Stalley 85, 94–7, 142, 170
Hugh Tait 86
Jean Tierney &
   Helen Mac Mahon 115
John Waddell 126, 128, 130
Richard Warner 125

FOREWORD

George Stacpoole, *Chairman, The Hunt Museum*

During the second half of the twentieth century, Ireland benefited from the donation of three major art collections. There was Sir Alfred Chester Beatty's extraordinary array of items from the Middle East, Asia, North Africa and Europe; the great paintings acquired by Sir Alfred Beit and John and Gertrude Hunt's eclectic mix, a collection based on a knowledge of art that was legendary. Over the years, with the benefit of an extraordinarily good eye, the Hunts put together an enchantingly diverse and extraordinary collection of art. This was all the more remarkable, in that, while Beatty and Beit were both wealthy, the Hunts were people of modest means, who none the less accumulated an art collection of high international esteem and range, from Neolithic Europe to the contemporary world.

The Hunts believed visual education to be of the utmost importance if people were to enjoy art and be educated by it. They were determined, therefore, that their collection should be exhibited in its entirety to the public and, with that in mind, they searched for a suitable location for its display. In the early 1970s Dr Edward Walsh offered them exhibition space at the University of Limerick, where part of the collection was displayed in 1978. When the eighteenth-century Limerick Custom House subsequently became available for alternative use, the prospect of a permanent home for the collection appeared feasible. With strong support from the Irish Government and the Office of Public Works, and under the firm guidance of chairman Dr Tony Ryan, the Hunt Museum's first director, Mairead Dunlevy (later succeeded by Jonathan Voak), was able to ensure a smooth transition for the collection from Limerick University to the Custom House, and the Museum opened its doors to the public on 14 February 1997.

John and Trudy Hunt, children of John and Gertrude Hunt, have perpetuated their parent's generosity by adding to the collection to build further an already strong collection of art. The benefit of this to the Irish nation, and in particular to the city of Limerick, cannot be overstated. In a relatively short period of time the Museum has managed to establish itself not only as one of Ireland's major museums but as one that is highly regarded in Europe and beyond. It would never have acquired this status without the assistance of its small but dedicated staff, and the considerable interest and goodwill of the public, aided by a thriving docent programme. Through the work of the docents it has been possible to provide an outstandingly good educational service, with several of the guides being individually expert in specific areas of the collection. The activity of the Friends of the Hunt Museum, including lectures, outings and fund-raising, has been of further advantage to the Museum.

When the decision was taken to publish this guide, a generous financial bequest, from a benefactor who wishes to remain anonymous, made it possible to offer it for sale at a vastly reduced price. All of us, here at the Museum and you the reader, are the beneficiaries of this act of great generosity.

INTRODUCTION

The Formation of the Collection and Foundation of the Hunt Museum

The Hunt Collection is an internationally important holding of approximately 2,000 works of art and antiquities, a personal collection that very much reflects the diverse tastes of John and Gertrude Hunt, who selected each piece according to the quality of its design, craftsmanship and artistic merit. These criteria were applied to objects from all periods of time: from the Stone Age to the twentieth century, from an Egyptian statuette to a Giacometti drawing, from Cycladic sculpture to Henry Moore.

In many ways the Hunt Collection is more an accumulation than a collection in the traditional sense, which the Hunts never intended as such to form. Its creation was less a deliberate policy of accumulation but more the result of their attention being diverted to different cultures, and then, as they became more secure in their circumstances, finding themselves acquiring pieces that reflected their developing interests and curiosity.

Curious they certainly were, for it was their shared love of the past that influenced their final decision to buy or not to buy each particular piece. Many objects, such as the coin of Syracuse, were acquired simply because the Hunts wanted to establish what exactly these artefacts were. Acquisition, in such circumstances, was less about ownership than the need to study something at close quarters until curiosity was satisfied.

John Hunt was born in England in 1900, of Irish parentage from counties Limerick and Clare. In his youth he studied architecture and medicine before applying his energies to the pursuit of his fascination with the past. He started his career as a dealer, with his antiques shop in London's Bury St achieving particular respect within the trade. Having become a particular authority on medieval art, John Hunt became an adviser to the British Museum, London; the Cloisters, part of the Metropolitan Museum of Art, New York; the Aga Khan; the Hearst Foundation and, most notably, Sir William Burrell. In later years he also advised Sotheby's, where both he and his wife, Gertrude, developed a close friendship with the then chairman Peter Wilson.

Gertrude Hunt was born in Mannheim, Germany, in 1903, where her grandfather was a senior civil servant. She met John Hunt in London in

The Hunts' Kitchen at Lough Gur, Co. Limerick in the 1940s

the 1930s, and it was there that their mutual interests helped form a bond between them that would keep them together until John's death in 1975.

The antiques market was thriving in London in the 1930s, and John and Gertrude Hunt were not alone in wanting to avail themselves of a fluid market and rapid turnover of quality pieces. European museums were concentrating their resources on restoring buildings damaged during the Great War, while those in North America, not yet fully endowed, had not entered the market in a meaningful way. Against this global backdrop the Hunts' business flourished, and within this context they held onto items that most dealers would have been tempted to sell.

By the early 1940s, the focus of their work shifted from that of shop-based dealers to a role as advisers to major collectors. This enabled them to leave London and set up home in Lough Gur, County Limerick. By then they had accumulated many of the objects that can be seen today in the Hunt Museum. However, their years in Lough Gur, and those following their move to Dublin in 1956, saw a shift in their pattern of acquisition. The transition to an advisory role had certainly given them the time to indulge their passion for collecting, but it was the move to a bigger home that proved the catalyst for them to broaden their interests from the archaeological and medieval to the later decorative arts.

Their arrival in Drumleck, the Hunts' Dublin home, coincided with a significant life change when in 1957 they adopted a son, John, and then the following year, their daughter, Trudy. The Hunts' enthusiasm for parenthood surpassed their celebrated enthusiasm for art and life in general, and as a result, their travelling decreased considerably, undertaken only when necessary and condensed into as brief a time span as possible. A concurrent reduction in John's advisory work happily coincided with the growth of his role as a consultant for Sotheby's. Although this required frequent short visits to London, its regularity enabled John to spend more time at home with his family.

This also had the advantage of allowing him to write more. Along with a series of articles on built heritage for the *Irish Times,* there was also a regular output of journal contributions. His greatest achievement, the result of many years' work, was the 1974 publication of *Irish Medieval Figure Sculpture*, with the assistance of Dr Peter Harbison, which remains the definitive study of stone tomb effigies from 1200 to 1600.

More time at home also meant that the Hunts could devote more energy to transforming Drumleck into the family home that would also serve as a suitable repository for their ever-growing collection. The house

The Hunts' sitting room at Lough Gur, Co. Limerick in the early 1940s

became a treasure trove, in which sacred medieval objects were placed in juxtaposition to baroque flamboyance and Neolithic functionalism. Coffee tables and sideboards, shelves and drawers, indeed every nook and cranny was filled with art. Its groupings were decided more by lateral aesthetics than typological classification, and with a bravado that owed more to theatrical gesture than the canons of formal museum display.

The Hunts felt that they could see objects with a keener eye if they were removed from their context. A single axe in a display case containing many examples was somehow mute. On the other hand, they would insist, that same axe attracted more curiosity and demanded greater attention when viewed, say, between objects of virtu on a medieval table. Of course, a characteristic feature of the Hunt display was that it was ever changing. Paintings, tapestries, sculptures and smaller objects were all continuously moved around the house, both to effect a change in nuance of the display in its entirety and, with luck, to stimulate fresh insight into a particular item.

While the Hunts as collectors were a most successful double act, irrespective of era or civilisation they had quite different approaches in their response to a particular object. If John was the scholar, who revelled in studying an item in all its technical detail, Gertrude was guided more by her 'sixth sense' or intuition. Hers was an immediate, if intangible,

John and Gertrude Hunt with their children, John and Trudy, c.1964

A view of the garden at Drumleck, Co. Dublin, early 1960s

approach that would instantly declare an object 'right' or 'wrong'. And while she was invariably correct, she would rarely be able to articulate why she had come to a certain conclusion. John, on the other hand, would spend ages examining an object with a magnifying glass, as he consulted and pored over the literature, until he felt confident enough to deliver his considered opinion. It was the diversity of their approach, of course, that provided the spark which kept alive their passion for the past. Each would consistently seek the other's opinion, and they would challenge each other, by way of gifts to one another, to 'tell me what you think of this'.

Gardening was another big passion. Like the house, the garden had elements of both the formal and the informal. If the lawns and terraces were the equivalent of the grand reception rooms, the vegetable garden and the woodland reflected the more informal atmosphere of kitchen and library. As with the house, the grand effect was just as important in the garden. Each area was designed both as an entity and as a prelude to the next. At the front of the house a sweeping lawn led down a slope to a large meadow, which was bordered by a vast bank of rhododendrons. At the other side of the house the design was more formal: steps flanked by columns led through a series of terraces culminating in the rose garden. Also, just as individual works of art were moved around the house, plants and shrubs were continuously relocated in the garden in a constant search for perfection. John and Gertrude equally enjoyed the ongoing quest to improve the house and gardens at Drumleck. Both, however, expressed

John Hunt's stand at an antiques' fair in London, 1930s

Interior of the Hunts' home in London during the mid 1930s

their enthusiasm in different ways. John was always the master planner, who came up with the ever-evolving grand design, while Gertrude adopted the hands-on role, positively revelling in getting her hands dirty.

If John were to follow suit, it was more likely to be in relation to archaeology, which, always of passing interest to him, became an abiding passion in the mid-1940s at Lough Gur. The plethora of ancient monuments around Lough Gur obviously enhanced its appeal, as did his growing friendship with the archaeologists excavating the sites there. While Gertrude fed the team, John rolled up his sleeves and joined in the excavations. He developed a particularly close friendship with Professor O'Kelly of University College Cork, who assisted Professor Ó Ríordán with the excavations at Lough Gur. Under Professor O'Kelly, John later completed an M.A. thesis on the subject of medieval armour and eventually began his own excavations at Clonroad More, County Clare, and Caherguillemore, County Limerick.

A turning point in John Hunt's life came when he decided to build a reconstruction of the Neolithic house at Lough Gur, with the sole aim of testing an interpretation of the excavated evidence. This was certainly a pivotal moment, and while he continued his principal role as adviser to collectors, the appeal of testing the archaeological evidence, through practical reconstruction in order to satisfy his sense of curiosity about how our forebears lived, began to take precedence. It was a fascination that led to his involvement with the restoration of Bunratty Castle, County Clare, the development of the Folk Park there, and the later reconstructions at Craggaunowen, also in County Clare.

John Hunt's passion for living reconstruction was great enough to persuade the owner of Bunratty Castle, Lord Gort, that he should restore it in such a way as to illustrate everyday life in a medieval Irish castle. On completion, the Castle was furnished with items acquired by John on behalf of Lord Gort. For its opening in 1960 John conceived the idea of celebrating the occasion with a meal composed from medieval recipes, little realising that the concept of medieval banquets would grow into the huge contribution to regional tourism that it is today.

The Folk Park at Bunratty came about by chance when a traditional thatched cottage was scheduled for demolition to make way for the runway at Shannon Airport. Acutely aware that rural Ireland was losing much of its traditional architecture, John arranged for the house to be dismantled stone by stone and rebuilt on the grounds of Bunratty. In the years that followed, other house-types threatened with destruction – such as a forge, the Golden Vale house and a fisherman's cottage – were all moved to Bunratty, creating there an archive of rural vernacular architecture.

While his reconstruction of the Neolithic house at Lough Gur had been

Exterior view of the Museum

Interior view of the Museum

a largely academic exercise, John Hunt's work at Bunratty Castle and Folk Park was more populist in intent. It was his way of lobbying for a greater appreciation and awareness of the past. It was this approach that motivated him when he purchased Craggaunowen in 1970.

Craggaunowen Castle was a sixteenth-century four-storey tower house, typical of a type of fortified home of late medieval Ireland. John and Gertrude devoted considerable energy to restoring it and furnished it with contemporary items, many of which are now in the Hunt Museum. However, their ambitions for what was then known as the Craggaunowen Project went way beyond the restoration of the Castle. Their dream was to tell the story of Irish habitation and everyday life. To this end they used all available archaeological evidence to reconstruct a Bronze Age crannóg (or lake dwelling) on Craggaunowen Lake. Further up the site at Craggaunowen they reconstructed a ringfort to illustrate the daily lives of small farming communities in Early Christian Ireland.

John Hunt died shortly after Craggaunowen opened to the public in 1975. Gertrude, however, remained deeply committed to their dream and oversaw the relocation to Craggaunowen of the St Brendan boat, in which Tim Severin followed the saints' route from Ireland to America, first in 1966 and again in 1977.

In the last years of John's life, he and Gertrude grew increasingly aware of the scale of their collection and became even more keen to keep it intact. They were fortunate, therefore, to meet Professor Patrick Doran of the newly established National Institution for Higher Education (NIHE), now the University of Limerick. Dr Edward Walsh, the Institute's President, immediately agreed to house a substantial part of the collection, albeit on a temporary basis. With Professor Doran as Honorary Curator, the first incarnation of the Hunt Museum opened in 1978 in a display designed by the architect Arthur Gibney.

The Irish Government had declined the offer of the collection, and the requirement to find an owner to take responsibility for it became ever more urgent. A resolution to this, which gave particular satisfaction to Gertrude and her children, John and Trudy, was to establish The Hunt Museums Trust to hold the collection and the property at Craggaunowen on behalf of the people of Ireland. The Trust, formed in 1974, is made up of individuals and representatives of local and national bodies.

Among the Trust's charges was the search for a location in the Limerick region for a permanent home for the collection. This was not to be an easy task. Ireland was in the grips of what seemed to be unremitting recession, which, indeed, had been the reason why the Irish Government had decided originally not to accept the collection. The search for a home was not made easier by the fact that its temporary base at NIHE was considered successful and attractive. The Institute was willing to continue to bear the cost of maintaining the display and later, in 1992, even transferred it to a more desirable setting, making any relocation to a permanent home even less of a priority.

Two events, one tragic, the other fortuitous, injected a new sense of urgency into the need to find a permanent home for the collection. When Gertrude suffered a serious stroke in 1993, although her children, John and Trudy, were able to care for her at home, and she continued to enjoy a (slowly diminishing) quality of life, her days of leading the Hunt Museums Trust and driving the search for a permanent home for the collection were effectively over. It was at this stage that Gertrude's children resolved to find a new base for their parents' art collection. To this end they persuaded the Trust to establish a new body, The Hunt Museum Ltd, the sole purpose of which was the establishment of a permanent home for the Hunt collection. Having discussed the matter with Gertrude, John and Trudy agreed that if the new company were successful in finding a permanent home for the Collection, the family would donate the balance of it to the Museum. Many of the most important pieces in the Hunt Museum today were among the additional items on offer, including the Leonardo Horse, the Mary, Queen of Scots, Crucifix and the pictures by O'Conor, Fagan, Renoir, Gauguin and Picasso.

The Hunt Museum Ltd, as established by the Hunt Museums Trust, at last provided the energetic spark required to fire the creation of the Hunt Museum as we see it today. Under the chairmanship of Dr Tony Ryan, this new body was one of the first public–private partnerships in Ireland, in which the University of Limerick, Shannon Development and Limerick Corporation were all represented, as were local businesses. Serendipity played a role too when the former Limerick Custom House was made available through the good offices of Limerick Corporation and the Office of Public Works.

The Office of Public Works indeed proved central to the successful transformation of the Custom House into the Hunt Museum. It was their architects who oversaw the restoration of the building and the installation of the equipment there that would bring the Museum facilities up to international standards. The internal design of the Museum's displays was conceived by Robin Wade & Partners, who came up with a design solution that complied with their brief from The Hunt Museum Ltd.

The idea was to devise a museum that reflected the unique nature of works of art that had been collected for and displayed in an informal domestic setting. The result is a presentation that sidesteps the traditional chronological narrative preferred by the majority of museums, in favour of a thematic display reflecting the atmosphere of a private house. Thus the units in which the art is exhibited are closer in feel to household cabinets and bookcases than to formal museum cases. Similarly, the drawers, filled with an apparently random selection of items, are intended to encourage a sense of anticipation and curiosity not always found in the ordered formality of some museum collections.

When the Hunt Museum was officially opened by An Taoiseach John Bruton on 14 February 1997, it was a moment of great celebration for the partners involved in its establishment, for the Friends of the Museum and for the docents. However, with Gertrude having succumbed to illness in March 1995, it was also a day that was tinged with sadness: neither John nor Gertrude Hunt had lived to see the realisation of their dream. None the less, the Hunt Museum ultimately stands as a monument to their enthusiasm, curiosity and generosity. It remains the extraordinary legacy of two remarkable individuals who, in a lifetime together, assembled a unique collection that can be enjoyed for posterity by the people of Ireland and their visitors alike.

List of Patrons

The Hunt Museum is part funded by the Department of Arts, Sport and Toiurism. The Hunt Museum would like to thank the following patrons of the museum for their ongoing support:

Founding Patrons

Aer Rianta, Shannon
Aerfi Ltd
Analog
Anglo Irish Bank Corporation plc.
Arup Consulting Engineers
Aughinish Alumina
Bank of Ireland
P.G. and Sheila Boland
Christopher & Mary Byrne
Clare County Council
Connolly Sellors Geraghty Fitt
Roger & Jean Downer
Dromoland Castle Hotel
élan
Friends of The Hunt Museum
GE Capital
Info-lab Ireland Ltd.
John Sisk & Son
Limerick City Council
Limerick County Council
Mall Holdings
Michael & Joan Houlihan
Molex International
RTE
Malachy Skelly
Dr. T. A. Ryan
Smurfit Group
Toyota Ireland

Patrons

Brooks Properties
Castle T. Furniture
CRH plc.
Fyffes
John Griffin & Sons
Patrick Hoare
Dr. Heather Holloway
Barry and Irene Macken
O'Mahony's Booksellers
O'Gorman Solicitors
Don O'Malley & Partners
J.J. O'Toole
Betty Ryan
Sarsfield Credit Union

A SELECTION OF
150 WORKS
FROM THE HUNT
COLLECTION

Paintings

Four Cats Menu Card, *Plat del Dia*

Spanish, Pablo Picasso,
*c.*1900
Wax and ink on paper,
H 45.5 × W 29
Accession no: MG 145

The little-known P. Ruiz Picasso, who signed this simple sketch (typically using the surnames of both parents until 1901, when he discarded Ruiz in favour of his mother's name alone), is arguably the most acclaimed artist of the twentieth century. The celebrated Four Cats café (from the Catalan *Els Quatre Gats*), for which this sketch is a menu card, served as a meeting place for avant-garde artists and intellectuals in turn-of-the-century Barcelona. The bohemian environment of the restaurant provided the stimulus that Picasso (1881–1973), then an aspiring artist, sought. His first one-man show, staged in the café in 1900, was an informal exhibition of unframed charcoal portraits tacked directly onto the wall with drawing pins.

This menu card designed specifically to promote the dish of the day, *Plat del Dia*, the name of which would have been inserted into the large blank space below the image, is light-hearted and animated. A plump waiter, sporting a white apron and money belt, is depicted holding the dish of the day in one hand and a bottle of wine in the other. The caricatural and stylised nature of the sketch, with its emphasised outline, shows the influence of art nouveau, and particularly the poster style, popular at the time and especially associated with Toulouse-Lautrec.

Te Nave, Nave Fenua

French, Paul Gauguin, *c.*1894
Watercolour monotype heightened
with brush and water-based colours,
and white chalk on japanned paper,
H 39.5 × W 24.5
Accession no: MG 147

Post-Impressionist Paul Gauguin
(1848–1903) is perhaps best known for his
colourful and stylised paintings of Brittany
and Tahiti. During his first visit to Tahiti
in 1891 he produced a romanticised
account of his travels, *Noa Noa*
(Fragrance), which he planned to publish
on his return to France. *Te nave nave fenua*
(The Delightful Land) is one of the images
intended to illustrate the publication.
Gauguin exhibited a painting of the
subject in Paris in 1893, which he then
adapted first as a print and then in a series
of drawings and monotypes. With the aim
both to shock and titillate, the painting
posits a confrontation of Christian and
Polynesian culture. The young nude girl,
with a flying lizard hovering beside her
face, is interpreted as a Tahitian Eve, a free
translation of the theme of temptation in a
tropical setting. Her sidelong glance
engages enigmatically with the monster.

In an oil painting of the subject the
lizard has dramatic red wings, mutated
here into a rose-tinted wash. Similarly,
the exotic landscape is reduced in this
monotype to a delicate composition of
horizontal grey lines that hint at the
fantastically foliated setting, highlighted
with touches of pink, mauve and blue
wash. The watercolour is signed, lower
left, with artist's stamp, 'PGO'.

An Atlantic Drive

Irish, Jack B. Yeats, 1944
Oil on canvas, H 35.5 × W 46
Accession no: TB 009

Jack B. Yeats (1871–1957), son of portrait painter, John Butler Yeats, and brother of the poet William, was born in London. Though he attended art school in London and spent the early years of his career both there and in Devon, he identified himself as the harbinger of a new national art for Ireland. The Sligo of their forebears, where they spent much of their youth, remained for him and William the most potent of symbols. His watercolours and early oils are painted in a strongly outlined, illustrative, often symbolic manner. Out of the small *plein air* landscapes grew the later

spontaneous style with its broken texture and direct application of separated colours, through which he achieved an international reputation. 'It fulfils my theory that there can be modern painting. Life above everything,' Sickert wrote to him in 1924.

In *An Atlantic Drive*, an evocation of travellers on a sidecar, Yeats combines his own familiarity with the vista at Mullaghmore, County Sligo, with an awareness of its perpetuity. The picture was originally exhibited at the Limerick City First Annual Exhibition of Fine Art, in the Goodwin Galleries, Limerick, in March 1944, and afterwards at Yeats' National Loan retrospective in Dublin in 1945.

Landscape

French, Pierre Auguste Renoir, *c.*1886
Watercolour with pen and ink and pencil
drawing on paper, H 18.5 × W 27.5
Accession no: L 001

By the 1880s, Renoir (1841–1919), one of
the most popular of the French
Impressionists, became increasingly
dissatisfied with its techniques. His lack of
formal training as an artist was a constant
source of concern to him, and he decided
to concentrate on re-learning methods of
drawing and painting. His letters record
his search for a solution to his technical
problems, and in one, to the dealer
Vollard, he describes how he 'had reached
the end of Impressionism and reached
the conclusion that he could neither paint
nor draw'.

This small sketch is typical of this period
of experimentation. Using pen and ink,

Renoir meticulously drew the clusters of
trees and bushes on the hillside. In the
foreground he has apparently sketched the
reeds at the edge of a pool and indicated
their reflection. The centre of the
composition is carefully developed with
brushstrokes of colour capturing the form
of the landscape, overlaid with more
refined strokes, blending greens, orange-
brown, yellow and grey-blue to model
delicate details in the trees. There is a
casual sense to his approach. The same
light-blue wash used to accentuate the
trees in the centre is lightly drawn across
the sky. Although dated *c.*1882 by his son
Claude in his *Souvenirs sur mon père*
(1948), this work seems to be characteristic
of the artist's later period of crisis.

SS Sebastian, Nicholas of Myra and Anthony of Egypt

German, late 15th or early 16th century
Tempera and gold leaf on wood,
H 178 × W 89
Accession no: HCP 002

Originally part of a late-medieval German altarpiece, this panel probably depicts three of the Fourteen Holy Helpers (*Vierzehnheiligen*), the subject of a popular devotion in Germany and central Europe. An excellent example of the genre, the saints are identified both by their names at the bottom of the panel and by their attributes, which allowed the illiterate to identify the figures. As well as being pierced by arrows, Sebastian is somewhat unusually depicted as the risen Christ with beard and open red mantle. This depiction appears to be peculiar to Germany, where he was invoked as protector against plague. Nicholas, Bishop of Myra, patron of sailors, merchants, bankers, children and prostitutes, carries three golden balls on his book, symbolising the dowries he provided for the daughters of an improvident Roman senator. Anthony of Egypt, a hermit, is identified by a tau cross on his robe and a pig. Exposed to hallucinogenic temptations in the desert, he was called upon to protect against illness caught from eating rye bread infested with fungus.

The faces are particularly well painted, suggesting the master painter was exposed to Renaissance influence. The figures, clothing and attributes are executed in the Gothic style by minor painters, as was the custom. The background is skilfully gilded to resemble a damask cloth of gold hanging.

Crucifixion

Italian, Bernardo Daddi, mid-14th
century
Tempera and gold on panel,
H 33 × W 21
Accession no: CG 012

The panel is attributed to either the school of Bernardo Daddi (*fl.* 1320–48) or Daddi himself, a pupil of Giotto, who ran a large workshop. The size of the panel indicates that it is perhaps part of a larger piece, and it was not uncommon in fourteenth-century Florence for a crucifixion scene to form the right-side panel of a diptych or triptych. It may have originally stood on the altar of a small chapel in a Franciscan church. The iconography of the crucified Christ, depicting angels catching blood from the wounds with chalices, is clearly Eucharistic; the body and blood of Christ would be consumed in the form of communion during the Mass said in front of the altar. Beside the cross the Virgin sinks in a swoon, supported by one of the holy women and St John the Evangelist.

The swoon of the Virgin, although not found in the Gospels, is frequently found in medieval art, made popular by the cult of the seven sorrows of the Virgin. At the other side of the cross stand the Roman centurion and the guards bearing sponge and spear. In crucifixion scenes like this, St Mary Magdalene is frequently depicted clutching the bottom of the cross. Here she is replaced by St Clare of Assisi (1193–1253) and a Franciscan friar. Their anachronistic presence at the Crucifixion transforms a narrative scene into a more devotional one; the viewer is invited to contemplate the occasion as they do.

God the Father

French, Nicolas Froment, mid- to late 15th century

Tempera and gold on panel, H 50 × W 42

Accession no: MG 032

The panel is attributed to Nicolas Froment (*fl.* 1450–90). Froment, born in Uzés, Picardy, was strongly influenced by the Netherlandish School, in particular by Rogier van der Weyden (*c.*1400–64) and Dirk Bouts (*c.*1415–75). His realism is especially notable in a triptych depicting the *Raising of Lazarus* (1461), now in the Uffizi, Florence, where a fly is visible on a tablecloth. He was patronised by René, Duke of Anjou, in the 1470s, and he lived in Aix-en-Provence where, in 1476, he executed his painting of *Moses and the Burning Bush* (Cathedral of St Sauveur, Aix-en-Provence). This panel depicts God the Father and probably formed part of a larger piece depicting the Trinity. The difficulties of representing three persons in one God had been largely resolved by the fifteenth century, although the church was still uneasy about how the theological complexities were rendered visible by artists. If this figure did form part of the Trinity, the composition was probably of the type made famous by Masaccio's *Trinity* (1425–8) in Florence, in which God the Father is depicted as elderly and bearded, with arms outstretched and enclosing the figure of his son on the Cross and the dove of the Holy Spirit.

Triptych: Painted Epitaph

German or Flemish, assembled after 1611
Oil on soft-wood Panels,
H 114.2 × W 43.3 + 89 + 47
Accession no: HCP 001

This painted epitaph honours the cleric shown in a variety of poses: on the outside praying before a crucifix, on the inside right wing preaching and on the left, among the saved. An inscription on the base records his death in October 1611. Painted epitaphs were a cheaper alternative to stone. Ludovicus Proost, described on the base as the inventor or designer, assembled the memorial, using works by at least two different artists. The outside and inner wings are probably from the same studio, while the central image is by a more expert hand. The left wing, inspired by Ezekiel 9, shows the saved being marked with the tau cross, an echo of Dürer's angels holding back the winds. The heavily framed central picture is based on the law and gospel paintings of Reformation artists such as Lucas Cranach. Moses, beside the brazen serpent, represents law and points to Christ, source of grace. Mary Magdalene represents sinners. The preacher uses

Pauline texts to emphasise the saving power of the Cross.

What makes this piece so interesting is not so much its artistic merit but its iconography, intended, in a period of religious ferment, as either Catholic or Lutheran. We know it was designed as a puzzle, because an animal-like figure – the devil – writes at a desk under the church, '*Clapt, clapt indi het snapt*', an old Dutch proverb meaning 'Hurrah! Hurrah! If you get this!'

Breton Woman

Irish, Roderic O'Conor,
c.1896–7
Oil on canvas, H 125.5 × W 91
Accession no: MG 140

This is the largest surviving picture by Roderic O'Conor (1860–1940) and his most ambitious canvas, completed during a sojourn at Rochefort-en-terre, a hilltop village in the Morbihan region of Brittany. The artist's previous base, the town of Pont-Aven, was fast becoming overrun with tourists. Rochefort, on the other hand, offered an unspoilt haven where he could replicate his friend Gauguin's quest for 'the primitive', without needing to feel regret for declining the latter's invitation to accompany him in 1895 to the South Seas. O'Conor's new works were characterised by a return to a more Impressionist idiom, combining an earthy palette with gestural brushwork. Gone were the fiery colours and thick ribbons of paint that marked him out in the early 1890s as a daring post-Impressionist. The present picture, with its sombre tonality and creamy handling of paint, has more in common with the early works of Manet. The impact of the figure is enhanced by placing her in profile against a nondescript background and instilling her with a sense of dignity and quiet purpose. The net result is to make a virtue of her humble origins. In effecting this transformation from the specific to the universal, O'Conor may have taken inspiration from Whistler's famous portrait of his mother seated, in profile, facing left; he might have viewed it at the Luxembourg Museum, Paris, where it was exhibited from 1891. It was purchased from Roland, Browse & Delbanco, London, by John Hunt.

Ideas for Boxwood Carving

English, Henry Moore,
c.1932
Watercolour, pen and ink
on paper, H 36.5 × W 27
Accession no: JB 011

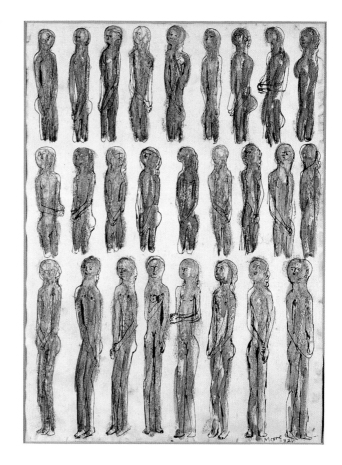

Henry Moore (1898–1986) was born at Castleford, Yorkshire, the son of an Irish coal miner and, of his generation, one of the most important sculptors in Europe. Moore won a scholarship to study art at Leeds in 1919 before going on to London's Royal College of Art. An early encounter with Roger Fry's *Vision and Design* (1920) initiated his deep interest in non-western art, particularly in pre-Colombian and African sculpture. The influence of such work and his knowledge of Modigliani, Brancusi, Epstein and later Picasso enhanced Moore's education. Moore's drawings are important in their own right, not simply as preparatory sketches for sculpture.

Ideas for Boxwood Carving, although very close to a sculpture executed the previous year, is one of many sheets that do not correspond to any known sculpture by Moore, but should be seen rather as visual notes. Moore described the body as the natural centre of his work, acknowledging its complexity and the exacting pressure it placed on the sculptor. Familiarity, he suggested, makes demanding critics of us. The three registers of figures on this sheet, two rows of three-quarter length and one row full length, seen largely in profile, reveal Moore's thorough investigation of an aspect of the body and his exploration of the many formal possibilities of that pose. It is signed 'Moore'32' on the bottom right.

The Artist and his Wife

English, Robert Fagan, 1803
Oil on canvas, H 66 × w 90
Accession no: MG 146

Robert Fagan (1761–1816) was born in London, where his father, a Corkman, was a baker. He is not known to have visited Ireland, but he regarded himself as Irish, none the less, and painted at least one patriotic portrait, that of Margaret Simpson as Hibernia. Fagan was educated at the Royal Academy School and afterwards travelled to Italy via Paris. He reached Rome in 1784 and lived there for most of his life. He painted portraits of grand tourists of outstanding quality and worked as a dealer and an archaeologist, initially at Ostia, Italy, and later in Sicily. He was subsequently appointed Consul General of Sicily and Malta in 1809.

This self-portrait with his second wife, Maria Ludovica' Flajani, whom he married in 1801, shows her *à la grecque*, a style fashionable on the continent, especially in Paris, and used to evoke classical Greece, whose democratic politics were then enormously admired. Fagan visited England in 1815 to paint murals on classical themes at Attingham Park, Shropshire, for Lord Berwick, whom he had met in Naples. On his return to Rome in 1816, a combination of ill health and financial reverses led to his suicide.

Seated Woman

Swiss, Alberto Giacometti,
c.1950
Pencil on paper, H 45 × W 31.5
Accession no: TB 008

This signed pencil sketch of a seated woman by the Swiss-born Alberto Giacometti (1901–66) is possibly a preparatory work for an ink-wash or oil painting. Although Giacometti is known primarily as a sculptor in plaster and bronze, in the late 1940s he applied himself equally to the creation of two-dimensional works. While other artists of the period were experimenting with abstraction, his work remained rooted in figuration. The emaciated, elongated figure sculptures, reminiscent of concentration camp victims, for which he is best known, encapsulated the post-Second World War existentialist philosophies of spiritual alienation, an outlook closely associated with Jean-Paul Sartre, whom Giacometti befriended in Paris in 1941.

It can be assumed that the model in this sketch is either Giacometti's mother or his wife, Annette Arm, both of whom frequently appear in his work. In a pose typical of Giacometti's later depictions of female figures, the subject is captured in a static seated posture; a strident, more forceful pose is generally reserved for the male figure. However, in Giacometti's two-dimensional works his favoured format for either sex is the lone, seated figure in a full-frontal, confrontational pose. In this drawing the figure, with hands clasped, is placed at a table in a sketchy interior. Despite the frenetic nature of the framework of linear detail about the subject, the overall mood is of calm resignation. It is signed 'Alberto Giacometti' on the bottom left.

Trompe-l'œil of a Letter-rack

English, attrib. Strickland
Lowry, 18th century
Oil on canvas, H 57 × W 47
Accession no: HCP 006

Trompe-l'œil was popular during the Renaissance and Baroque periods. It alludes to the illusionist effect of simulating three-dimensional objects on a two-dimensional surface. Samuel van Hoogstraten's (1627–78) Trompe-l'œil of a letter-rack of 1670 in the Kunsthalle, Karlsruhe, Germany, depicting letters and jewellery secured by tape to a board, is a precedent for this picture. Strickland Lowry (1737–85) was an important painter of trompe-l'œil in eighteenth-century Ireland. Born in Whitehaven, Cumbria, he worked in Staffordshire, Shropshire, Dublin and particularly the north of Ireland. He is known to have completed three trompe-l'œil paintings of engravings pinned to boards: Reynolds' mezzotint of the first Duke of Leinster, Nathaniel Hone's Spartan Boy, and a third, entitled Lowry, a possible self-portrait, are clearly related to this work. A tentative attribution of this picture to Lowry is based on the style of these, together with a still-life of a violin, sheets of music and a flute, signed and dated '1776'. His earliest documented portrait in Ireland, that of the Cobbe children of Newbridge, is dated 1765, while his Leinster mezzotint was published in 1775. The envelope in this work, inscribed 'To Mrs. Grady at Elton', probably refers to Mary Hungerford, who married Standish Grady in 1737. The family owned Elton in east Limerick and were living in Cappercullen (now Glenstal) in 1759. It would be tempting to suggest that the sportsman in the watercolour was a Grady!

Abstract Figures

English, Henry Moore, 1932
Chalk, crayon and watercolour on paper,
H 37.5 × W 54.5
Accession no: MG 143

Henry Moore (1898–1986) was probably the most controversial artist in Britain when he executed this drawing. The strongly abstract nature of his work met with much opposition, but this did not prevent Moore's appointment as an official war artist from 1940 to 1945. It was in 1940 that he began his most famous series, the *Shelter Drawings*, his tribute to the people of London during the blitz.

This work incorporates many of Moore's most abiding concerns: the human body, his preference for organic, bony shapes, the use of the hole or cavity in the body and, in this drawing, his emerging interest in placing the figure in a landscape. The open cavity in the central figure was to become a hallmark in Moore's work. He often thought of the body as a shell, or container, and constantly reiterated the sculptural importance of the negative as well as the positive space. Typically, these drawings do not correspond to any single piece of finished sculpture, but the central figures contain references to *The Helmet* (1940) in Much Hadham and the later totemic figures of the 1950s and 1960s. The small size of the head in the two central figures is also typical of his work. It is signed 'Moore '32' on the bottom right.

View of Kilmallock, County Limerick

Irish, attrib. John George Mulvany, RHA,
c.1820–30
Oil on canvas, H 102 × D 153.5
Accession no: HCP 05

This view of the Anglo-Norman town of
Kilmallock with its picturesque ruins
reflects the nineteenth-century fascination
with antiquarianism and contemporary
interest in landscape painting, previously
regarded as an inferior art form. Mulvany
(c.1766–1838), landscape and genre
painter, employs the language of the
classical landscape formulated principally
by the French painter Claude Lorrain
(1600–82), and adapts it to an Irish
context by depicting medieval rather than
classical ruins. In the middle ground
Kilmallock's thirteenth-century landmarks
can be seen with King John's Castle in the
distance and the collegiate church with its
pre-Norman round tower and the ruined

Dominican priory, built outside the walled
town on the far right. The landscape is
enlivened by the rural genre scene in the
foreground. Following the tradition of
Claude, Mulvany employs compositional
devices, such as the bridge and river, to
lead the viewer from one horizontal plane
to the next, all unified by the fine tree
specimen dominating the foreground.

Mulvany painted in a similar style to
that of his younger brother Thomas James,
and the brothers rarely signed their work.
Their landscapes, characterised by a
smooth finish, soft pink tones and the
inclusion of charming pastoral scenes, are
particularly difficult to differentiate. Both
of the brothers studied in Dublin Society
schools and were nominated as founding
members of the Royal Hibernian
Academy, where they were regular
exhibitors.

Ceramics

Charlemont Dinner Service Plates

Chinese, 1793–4
Porcelain, Diam. 24.8
Accession nos: HCL 058; 059

Very few recorded, blue-and-white Chinese porcelain, armorial dinner services are known to have been produced for Irish families in the eighteenth century. One such service was made for James Caulfield (1728–99), fourth Viscount Charlemont, who was created earl in 1763 and elected Commander-in-Chief of the Irish Volunteers in 1780. In 1788, Charlemont, Ireland's most important patron of art and architecture in the second half of the eighteenth century, who became the first President of the Royal Irish Academy on its foundation in 1785, had helped one William Burroughs obtain a post with the East India Company. Burroughs arrived in

India in 1789 and rapidly rose up the judicial ranks. In March 1794 he wrote to Charlemont to say that, as a gift to his patrons, he had commissioned two dinner services from China, 'in their best Blue and White only'.

The dishes are beautifully executed in underglaze blue on a white ground. The border depicts the collar and badge of the Order of St Patrick, founded in 1783 as Ireland's only order of chivalry, with Charlemont among its 15 founder knights. The centre depicts the arms of Caulfield, with an earl's coronet and supported by two dragons. The Caulfield motto, *Deo Duce, Ferro Comitante* (God my Leader, Sword my Companion), is cited underneath. The service was dispatched to Ireland in 1794.

Belleek Candelabrum, 'Stag's Head'

Irish, Belleek, 2nd period mark,
c.1895
Porcelain, H 41.5 × w (of antler)
32 × D (of base) 20.5
Accession no: HCL 057

The Belleek pottery, founded in 1857, started making utilitarian articles to designs influenced by one of its founders, Robert William Armstrong, architect for the Worcester Royal Porcelain Works. A few years after its inception the pottery began to make finer ware, leading to a gold medal in 1865 at the Dublin International Exposition and, by 1869, Queen Victoria's patronage. Belleek became highly profitable, which enabled it to employ first-rate potters such as William Bromley and William Wood Gallimore, both of whom had worked for William Henry Goss of Stoke on Trent.

This piece was possibly a response to late Victorian interest in all things Scottish. The rise of the stag as a symbol of Scotland was popularised by Landseer's *Monarch of the Glen* (1851), in which Landseer typically used the Highlands of Scotland as a backdrop. The creator of the candelabrum is unknown. Elements of the design may be found elsewhere in other Belleek pieces, including the amphora lamp and the sea-urchin candleholders. It was probably designed to stand in front of a mirror. This unique piece belonged to the Condon family of Ballyshannon, avid collectors of Belleek, who were often given first choice of new pieces. It is tempting to think that this might be one of them.

Dish (with Crowned Woman Design)

Spanish, 13th century
Ceramic, Diam. 38.5
Accession no: MG 109

This large, deep, funnel-shaped dish with a narrow base and foot-ring is decorated with a striking portrait, expertly painted in broad, swift strokes, of a woman wearing a crown with an elaborate foliated crest. Foliage flanks her face, in which her eyes and eyebrows are particularly sizeable and prominent, and connects to a circular border. A band of diagonal strokes decorates the rim, with the overall design simple but expressive. Only the inside of the dish is glazed, the decoration painted in a pale greenish-blue colour.

Similar dishes are often thought to have been used as shop signs and incorporated as such into the walls of buildings, with those adorned with portrait heads and busts (of sirens, acrobats, women with fish and mirrors), said to represent courtesans. Others, differently decorated, can still be found set into the walls of Italian and Spanish churches. Traces of lime mortar on the reverse and rim indicate that this particular dish was once recessed in a wall, though other such dishes of similar type, in general use from the late twelfth century and throughout the thirteenth, would have been more domestic and decorative in function.

Maiolica Drug Jar (*albarello*)

Italian, Faenza or Venice, *c.*1510–20
Tin-glazed earthenware,
H 19 × w (at base) 12.5
Accession no: HCM 291

The *albarello* shape is of Islamic origin, popular in Italy in the fifteenth century and used to store spices and drugs. This jar has a squat, slightly waisted, cylindrical body, a sloping narrow band to a rolled foot that bears the St Bernardino rays and a narrow sloping shoulder to a short flared rim decorated with a zigzag pattern. It is painted dark blue and ochre on a white ground, and inscribed 'COMIN (S?)' in a white band at the centre front. Ornamental patterns of stylised flowers on thin coiling stems, surrounded by clusters of small dots, complete the decoration on the front. The reverse also bears these thin coiling stems but with stylised pinecones (a form of the Persian palmette) with ochre centres.

This type of decoration is very similar to that found on fifteenth-century Spanish imports. The inscription suggests it was intended as a store for cumin, an umbelliferous plant, the aromatic seeds of which were used both medicinally and as a spice in the Middle Ages. Indigenous to Upper Egypt, from early on cumin was also cultivated in other Mediterranean countries. The dried (*siccus*) fruit or seed was dispensed as a corrective for flatulence and as a remedy for colic and dyspeptic headache.

Maiolica Drug Jar

Italian, Venice, workshop or style of
Domenico da Venezia, *c.*1550–80
Tin-glazed earthenware,
H 29 × W (at base) 13
Accession no: HCM 290

This is a broad oviform jar painted
in a strong foliate design of pale
blue, orange, yellow, green, brown
and white against a dark-blue
ground. The decorative pattern
includes the flowers and leaves of
the acanthus with large and small
white flowers and berries. White
incised flourishes, created by drawing
a sharp implement through the blue
glaze, expose the white tin glaze
(sgraffito). The escutcheon on the
front, bearing the dedication 'IHS'
surmounted by a cross and three nails
(crucifixion), is surrounded by a blue
band with the straight and wavy lines of
St Bernardino. Around this, a white
band bears the emblem of the Jesuits,
'SOCIETAS.IESV+' (Society of Jesus).
'OXYMEL SINP', written on a white
decorative band below, refers to a
medicinal drug composed of vinegar
and honey, an old-fashioned remedy
for colds and sore throats.

In 1570 Camillo I Gonzaga
invited the Jesuits to build a
monastery with a school and
pharmacy, at Novellara, Reggio
Emilia. Today an extensive
collection of pharmacy jars with the
Jesuit emblem is housed there in the
Gonzaga Castle Museum, two of which
are of similar shape and decoration to
this example. Perhaps this jar is part
of a group, made in Venice, for the
pharmacy. A similar jar in the Palais
Lascaris, Nice, is attributed to Novellara.

Bronze Age Funerary Pottery

Tripartite Bowl Food Vessel

Irish, 2000–1700 BC
Clay, H 14 × Diam. (ext.) 14.5
Accession no: HCA 608

Incised-groove Vase Food Vessel

Irish, 2000–1700 BC
Clay, H 12.5 × Diam. (ext.) 14.1
Accession no: HCA 609

These clay containers are Early Bronze Age funerary pottery, known as 'Food Vessels'. Some nineteenth-century anti-quarians surmised that they were made to carry food to sustain the dead on their journey to the afterlife. Scientific analyses of residue indicate that some vessels contained porridge or ale. Usually found in stone-lined cist graves and associated with either cremations or interments, such vessels and other grave goods, particularly bronze daggers, suggest a high social status of the dead. The vessels were made by coiling clay and baking it in open fires. The bowl is similar to Scottish food vessels, while the vase may be an insular Irish tradition.

The largely intact tripartite bowl (HCA 608) has a bevelled rim with impressed comb decoration; its external surface is divided into three zones by two cordons or raised bands, decorated with triangular motifs. Either incised or comb-stamp lines decorate each zone. There are incised horizontal grooves immediately under the rim, with a band of vertical grooves below this. There is an area of vertical grooving in the middle of the vessel and horizontal comb-impressed lines on the lower section. There are lime accretions on the vessel surface.

The vase (HCA 609) has an angular profile and is decorated entirely with incised grooving. While a herringbone motif rings the internal rim, the external decoration is zoned. There is a vertical ladder pattern on the rim/neck; a band of alternate vertical and horizontal panels on the shoulder with a herringbone design beneath, and the lower body has infilled chevron patterning with a herringbone motif on the lower section. In the base of the vase there is a circular hole.

Gilded *Bourdaloue*

French, 18th century
Ceramic, L 20 × W 10.8 × D 10.4
Accession no: DG 101

A *bourdaloue* is an eighteenth-century slipper-shaped lady's urinal. Often hidden away in a muff when travelling, it was sometimes known as a coach pot. It took its more general name from a Jesuit father, one Louis Bourdaloue, whose interminably long sermons, preached at Versailles, were extremely popular, especially with the ladies of the court. In order not to miss one word of them, it was necessary for the congregation to arrive several hours beforehand to secure a seat, which could not be vacated lest it be immediately reoccupied, creating a situation that was tailor-made for the *bourdaloue*.

The earliest surviving examples, made at Delft, date from 1710, but most were made between 1725 and 1770. They were manufactured in French and German factories such as Chantilly and Meissen as well as in China and Japan for export. In England the earliest were made in the London district of Bow, *c.*1750, and later at Derby, Caughley and Chamberlains Worcester. Wedgwood made them of creamware. Many were delicately decorated and have been mistaken for sauceboats! This example is heavily gilded and decorated in the French Empire style. Most factories produced them in porcelain, though occasionally they were made in faience, silver or japanned metal.

Maiolica Pharmacy Jar

Italian, Florence region, ?Montelupo,
1560–80
Tin-glazed earthenware,
H 39.2 × W (at base) 14
Accession no: HCM 293

This jar must have been made for a
Franciscan pharmacy. It may have
contained a liquid drug or an aromatic
water or syrup. Religious houses were the
main providers of medicines in the
sixteenth century. In Tuscany alone there
may have been as many as 100 Franciscan
friaries, each with its own pharmacy, so it
is impossible to say for which particular
pharmacy this jar was made. This large
drug jar has an inverted baluster body and

a short neck with two handles moulded in
the form of sea horses or dragons, with a
pouring spout on the upper shoulder. It is
painted in dark blue, green, orange, yellow
and black. A roundel on the front, bearing
the arms of the Franciscans, is surrounded
by a scrolling frame with a putto's head.
Azure, a cross of Calvary, above a mount of
six summits, mounted by two stigmatised
human hands, saltire, argent and purpure,
the dexter hand with three rays issuing
from the palm. The reverse is decorated
with stylised pinecones in blue on a white
ground, a form of the Persian palmette.
The jar may have had a lid, now lost.

Julia and Ottavio Figures

Bavarian, Nymphenburg, modelled by
F. A. Bustelli, late 18th century
Hard-paste porcelain, H 19 – H 18.7
Accession nos: MG 106A; 106B

Franz Anton Bustelli (1723–63) was known for his energetic, witty and graceful figures created at Nymphenburg, Bavaria. Although porcelain shrinks during firing, his pieces have a sculptural quality, each frozen in a theatrical pose, an elegant turn. His control and manipulation of hard-paste porcelain is shown in the crisply detailed clothing, hair, out-raised hands and facial expression. One of Bustelli's most famous sets of figures was based on the Italian *commedia dell'arte*. Acted by troupes of strolling players, it was so popular that engravings of the characters were published from 1729 onwards. Contemporaries knew the personality of each of these figures, and their role in intrigue and seduction. Apart from the main protagonists, there were courtiers or serious characters such as Julia and Ottavio. The Nymphenburg pottery faced financial crises from 1767, and highly marketable figures such as these consequently continued in production after Bustelli's death.

Julia and Ottavio at the Hunt Museum are of hard-paste porcelain with a high feldspathic glaze. They differ greatly in weight. The heavier, Julia, is impressed simply with a circle, in contrast to Ottavio's small Nymphenburg shield of 1765–80. Slight variations on the figures from Bustelli's period include the much thinner and more sweeping rococo bases, together with tiny modifications in dress detail and hairstyles, all of which suggest a dating in the late eighteenth century.

Apulian Red-figured *Lebes Gamikos*

Greek, second half 4th century BC
Clay, H 19.3 (with handles)
Accession no: HCM 234

The *lebes gamikos* is a distinctive Greek wedding vessel, believed to have been a gift for the bride. Before the fourth century BC it was usually attached to a tall stand instead of the foot. This vase has a slim body and two upright handles. The lid has an elongated finial. There is a decoration of rays on the shoulder, bands of wave pattern beneath the scenes and around the lid, and composite palmettes below the handles. There are different scenes on each side of the body. On one, a woman seen in left profile, seated on a rock, cradles a dish. On the other, a winged Eros, similarly posed, clutches a mirror in his right hand. There are flowers in the field, and abundant use has been made of added yellow and white colour. In representations of wedding scenes the *lebes* is shown to contain branches of myrtle, evocative of fertility and joy; any other use on such occasions is unknown. Like other bridal vases, the *lebes gamikos* also had a funerary function, particularly in connection with girls who died unmarried. The finest Athenian *lebetes* often depict wedding scenes, but the Apulian examples of the later fourth century bear the kind of non-specific and trivial iconography found on this example.

Attic White-ground *Lekythos*

Greek, Tymbos Workshop, second quarter
5th century BC
Clay, H 19
Accession no: HCM 228

The *lekythos* is a characteristic type of
Greek oil container. It was known by the
same name in ancient times, although the
word was also used to refer to other types
of oil vessel. The narrow neck and cup-
shape mouth ensured that its precious
contents poured slowly. The technique
used to decorate this *lekythos* is known as
'white-ground', so called because it
involved painting the body of the vase with
a slip of pure clay that provided a white
background for the scene. Being buried
ceremonially with the dead, particularly
from the second quarter of the fifth
century BC, white-ground *lekythoi* had a
specifically funerary use in Athens and
were therefore painted predominantly
with funereal scenes.

The Tymbos workshop, to which this
vase is attributed, produced a large
number of small white-ground funerary
lekythoi. The scene on this piece is painted
in golden-brown glaze paint. A single
figure, a woman, in right profile, dressed
in Greek *chiton* and *himation*, is shown
approaching a tomb that is marked by a
stele (gravestone) with a gabled top. She
holds out a garland in her right hand. Two
(faded) red ribbons are wrapped around
the *stele*. Offering leafy wreaths or garlands
and hanging coloured ribbons from tombs
were typically Greek rites associated with
the cult of the dead.

Faience Pilgrim Flask

?French, Nevers, tin-glazed earthenware,
17th century
H 24 × W (at base) 12
Accession no: MG III

This jar is moulded in the form of a pilgrim flask with four looped handles and a narrow neck. It is decorated in blue, green and yellow on a white background. A circle, surrounded on two sides by a scallop-shell decoration, shows a bishop saint in alb and cope, wearing a mitre and pectoral cross. He carries a crosier in his left hand, and his right is raised in blessing. The background is painted with foliage and features two volcanic hills. A similar circle on the reverse is painted with foliage, a white flower and a yellow tulip. Blue gadrooning and tulip-like motifs decorate the neck. The ceramic, pilgrim-flask form reflects the influence of metal pilgrim flasks patterned after the dried gourds used to carry water, which were suspended from the neck or the waist by side loops.

At the end of the sixteenth century, the most successful of the early factories in France, Nevers, came under the Italianate influence of the partnership between the Gambin (Faenza) and Conrade (Savona) families. The latter had a privilege from Henri IV that gave them the sole right to produce pottery in Nevers for 30 years. Early in the seventeenth century devotional figures as well as white-ground wares (*faïence blanche*) were produced in the new compendiario style.

Plastic Vessel in the Form of a Hand

Greek, ?5th–4th century BC
Clay, H 9.5 × W 7.6
Accession no: HCM 233

The shape of this container, most probably for perfumed oil, is unparalleled among Greek vases. It is moulded in the form of a hand clasping a miniature oil jar (*lekythion*), the smallest of the vase shapes produced by Greek workshops in the Classical period. The hand is painted white, a Greek convention to indicate that it is female. The *lekythion*, painted black, has a tall neck and a mouth with a broad overhanging rim and small opening for filling and pouring. In spite of its uniqueness, the hand vase belongs none the less to a category of Greek vessels known as 'plastic vases'. The most common and attractive of these are the so-called head vases, which are jugs or drinking cups with bodies in the shape of moulded human or animal heads. Rarer versions include vases made in the form of feet, shells or small animals, and some even more unusual ones are modelled on whole figures holding vases, a type to which the hand vase is likely to be most closely related.

Raqqan-style Bowl

Syrian, 13th century
Stone paste, H 7.5 × W 17.5
Accession no: MG 130

During the seventh century, Islam spread rapidly. Potters' work reveals links with the artistic traditions of countries that were gradually absorbed into the Islamic world as well as those that merely came into contact with it. The conquering Arabs had a powerful empire, which extended from Persia in the east to the Iberian peninsula in the west. As a consequence, Islamic pottery shows very rich and diverse influences. Techniques, including lustreware, tin glazing and underglaze painting, were invented by Islamic potters and artists. Potteries in the Near East, including Raqqa in northern Syria, were prolific during the twelfth and thirteenth centuries.

This bowl has many characteristics of Raqqan ware, including its conical shape with straight sides and rim. The ceramic body is stone paste or fritware, a composite of white clay, ground quartz and powdered glass. It is largely unglazed on the exterior, and its body is coarse and sandy. The clear alkaline turquoise glaze has been applied so thickly that it has pooled in the centre of the base and dripped unevenly down the outside rim. The glaze is crazed and has become iridescent due to the salt content in the soil in which it was buried. The simple shape and decoration indicate this bowl was produced for daily use.

Silver-gilt Mounted Chinese Bowl

Chinese, 16th–17th century
Porcelain, H 13.5 × W 21.5
Accession no: DG 098

The export of porcelain from China increased steadily during the reign of the Ming Emperor Wan Li (1573–1619). A turning point in Chinese ceramics was the production of Kraak porcelain, so-called after the ships, known as carracks, that brought it to Europe. Blue and white was produced in massive quantities, almost exclusively for export. Porcelain with European silver-gilt mounts was extremely popular in Elizabethan England. The gilded mounts provided both protection for the fragile porcelain and adornment to special pieces. The decoration of masks and caryatids was introduced in drawings by Hans Holbein the Younger (1497–1543).

This bowl is porcelain, a mixture of kaolin and china stone. The decoration on the bowl is cobalt underglaze. Divided into panels on the outside, with flying horse motifs on the top, there are sprays of flowers and berries underneath. The inside centre circle depicts a landscape scene, and above this there is a circle of intertwined flowers, the cakra or flaming-wheel motif, with the top panel on the inside rim decorated with pagodas, seascapes and landscapes. The Shou Fu seal mark is on the base. Chinese porcelain was highly prized, and Queen Elizabeth I is reputed to have given a similar piece to her godchild Sir Francis Walsingham, which now resides in the Metropolitan Museum of Art, New York.

Pietà

German, Meissen, *c*.1732
White porcelain, H 55 × W 29 × D 17
Accession no: JB 009

The nature of the material used in this piece confirms that the Pietà was made at the Meissen porcelain factory, established near Dresden in 1710 by Fredrick-Augustus I, Elector of Saxony, following the discovery of the secret of making hard-paste porcelain, previously known only in Asia. Augustus had a passion for collecting porcelain and was the first European ruler to control the production of true porcelain. Although made at Meissen in Protestant Saxony, the Pietà is untypical of Meissen figure sculpture. It is a piece of Catholic baroque art, a reminder that the elector (and his heir) had converted to Catholicism for political reasons. The palaces that Augustus had built to house his porcelain collection included a chapel, and records show that

Calvary figures were made for it.

The quality of the modelling in the Pietà suggests that it may be the work of J. J. Kändler, the outstanding Meissen modeller. Kändler trained as a sculptor under Benjamin Thomae, court sculptor at Dresden, before coming to Meissen in 1731. In terms of expression and modelling, the Pietà resembles Thomae's Apostle John, modelled for Meissen *c*.1719. The pathos expressed by the heavenward gaze of the Mother of God, who reveals the limp body of her dead son to the devout spectator, is designed to arouse religious ardour in the faithful.

Serving Dish with Butterflies and Beetles

German, Meissen, *c.*1820
Porcelain, L 39:5 × w 29
Accession no: HCL 060

This large serving dish comes from a
service of more than 100 pieces commissioned by General Sir Richard Bourke,
KCB, of Thornfields, Lisnagry, from the
Meissen factory in 1820. The dish is white
porcelain with a reddish-brown rim, and is
decorated with three large and two smaller
coloured butterflies and two coloured
beetles. The Bourke crest, a collared and
chained mountain cat (*sejeant guardant*),
adorns its centre just below the rim.
On the back are crossed swords, the mark
of the Meissen factory, in underglaze blue.

The service was used by Sir Richard on
first becoming Governor of the Cape
Colony of South Africa in 1824. He then
used it later, between 1831 and 1837, in
Australia, where he was one of the
founders of the city of Melbourne and
where two streets preserve his family
name and that of his wife, Elizabeth. Sir
Richard returned to Limerick in 1840,
where he served as High Sheriff. He died
in 1855 and is buried at Castleconnel,
County Limerick.

Snuff-box

German, Meissen, 1st third 18th century
Porcelain, L 8 × w 6 × D 3.2
Accession no: DG 002

This small porcelain snuff-box has a hinged lid attached by means of a silver-gilt frame. Snuff-boxes were objects of luxury in the eighteenth century, and many were painted by artists of note at the principal porcelain factories. This box is too large to be carried in the pocket and may have been used at table. Wearing on the periphery of the glaze, on the bottom, is evidence of sliding or passing of the box. The decoration was probably the work of Johann Georg Heintze, who had been apprenticed to J. G. Herold, a master painter at the Meissen factory. Herold introduced the muffle kiln, a cooler furnace better suited to firing coloured enamels. In Janet Gleeson's *The Arcanum* it is said that Heintze painted scenes of Arcadian landscapes and harbour views, in which an obelisk provides a reliable sign of his authorship. The existence of obelisks and harbour scenes on this box is surely enough evidence to attribute the enamelling to Heintze.

Snuff reached the western world from North America, and its introduction to Europe via France in 1561 was due to Jean Nicot, the French ambassador to Portugal from 1559 to 1561, whose name is preserved in that of the plant *herba Nicotiana*, Nicot's plant, species *Tabacum*.

London-type Baluster Jug with Rouen-style decoration

English, 13th century
Lead-glazed earthenware,
H 23.7 × W 18.5 × D 16.5
Accession no: CG 054

This handsome jug is of a type made in
London in the thirteenth century as a
direct imitation of smaller jugs from
Rouen. As the clay used in Rouen was
white, the application of a brown slip gave
the characteristic brown and yellow finish.
In contrast, the body colour of the London
type was a dull reddish brown, which
meant a white slip clay had to be applied
between the clay and the lead glaze to
achieve the bright yellow finish. On this
jug, the area for decoration was clearly
defined, leaving the rim, handle and
base in the original dull red.
The lack of a spout may
seem odd, but in fact the
jug functions very well
for pouring or even
for drinking straight
from the pot!

Jugs were the main vessels of the
medieval period when many of them,
along with plates and mugs, were made of
wood or leather (for the poor) or in pewter
and other metal (for the wealthy). It is
possible that the development of this kind
of decoration resulted from the loss of
Normandy by King John in 1204, and the
resultant cessation of imports from
Rouen. Both Rouen- and London-type jugs
are rare finds in Irish excavations as the
French material came primarily from the
wider Bordeaux region.

Rose-type Watering pot

?English, Tudor period
Lead-glazed earthenware,
H 31.7 × W 28.7 × D 20.5
Accession no: HCM 243

This sixteenth-century watering pot is essentially a jug with a rose or sprinkler attached to the shoulder and a guard over part of the rim. The rod handle was affixed to the pot with three thumb marks, and the guard was decorated with overlapping ridges of clay and a thumbed edge. The pot was made of an orange-brown clay with a lead glaze containing copper, which gave a green to brown finish. The glaze was unevenly applied, primarily on the belly or bib.

While watering pots of this period were more in the style of modern watering cans, medieval watering pots were shaped like bottles with holes in the base. These vessels were designed for watering plants, but they were also used for sprinkling water on earthen floors to settle the dust in hot dry weather, and some wealthy houses also had watering pots in metal. An Irish reference of 1343 mentions the purchase of 'a "spoucher", bought to throw water for making the walls', costing one and a half pence, and this may be a medieval name for a watering pot.

Siegburg Baluster Jug with Silver-gilt Mounts

German, ?workshop of Christian Schnulgen,
c.1550–80
White salt-glazed stoneware,
H 24 × W 13 × D 10
Accession no: MG 077

Pottery production in the town of
Siegburg, east of Bonn, flourished from
the late twelfth to the mid-seventeenth
century. This jug is typical of the highly
decorated pieces of the later sixteenth
century and shows the influence of the
Renaissance. The upper body is decorated
with vertical carved diaper or diamond
pattern, and the lower body with vertical
gadrooning or fluting. The neck
decoration consists of an applied, moulded,
frieze band of cherubs and hearts.
The strap handle was attached to the body
prior to the decoration and has a distinctive 'twist in the tail'. The embossed
silver-gilt mount dates to the 30-year
period 1550–80, contemporary with the
production of the pot.

While a specific name has been
associated with this pot, it may refer in fact
to the mould maker rather than a potter's
workshop. The work of the Siegburg
stoneware potters was highly regulated
with a seven-year apprenticeship and strict
enforcement of rules to retain the secrecy
of the production methods. All German
stonewares are found in large quantities in
England, but this type of vessel is rarely
excavated in Ireland.

Frechen Mug with Silver-gilt Mounts

German, late 16th century
Salt-glazed stoneware, H 16.1 × W 11.5 × D 10
Accession no: CG 025

Stoneware potteries in the centre of
Cologne developed from the earthenware
potteries, but the required high firing
temperatures, the poisonous fumes and
the increased consumption of domestic
fuel led to the expulsion of the stoneware
potters to the town of Frechen, some
10 km to the south-west, who took their
designs and moulds with them. The glossy
finish on the pots was achieved by adding
salt to the kiln at a certain stage in the
firing process, and the so-called tiger glaze
on this vessel was highly prized in itself.

The British preference for adding
precious mounts to undecorated
stonewares is well illustrated by this
Frechen mug or tankard.

The mount may also be contemporary with
the date of the pot as the later sixteenth-
century fashion was for engraved mounts,
less exuberant than earlier embossed
ones. During the period of the English
Civil War (1642–51), many such mounts
were removed from the vessels and melted
down for use in the War. Dutch and
German fashion generally tended to
decorate the jugs with pewter mounts
rather than silver or silver gilt, and many
of these may be seen in the contemporary
paintings of artists such as Pieter Brueghel
(1564–1638). The *Bartmann* or bearded-
man jugs are the best-known vessels from
the Frechen area, and these are sometimes
associated with coin hoards
or seen as witch bottles.

Wine or Brandy Delftware Barrel

Irish, Dublin, c.1755–65
Delftware, l 30.2
Accession no: HCL 031

This large Dublin delftware barrel, which would have rested originally on a wooden cradle, was used in the mid-eighteenth century for dispensing wine or brandy. Only five Irish delftware barrels are known, and this landscape-decorated example – one of a pair – is certainly among the finest to have survived. The crest on each end indicates that it was commissioned by the Molyneux family of Castle Dillon in County Armagh. The imaginary landscapes, painted freehand on either side, are typical of the very best of Dublin delftware.

Historically, all such landscapes were attributed to the Irish artist Peter Shee, known to have worked at the Dublin pottery during the 1750s and 1760s, but marks recorded on surviving examples now suggest that at least five different painters were involved in their manu-facture. (More recently the name of Robert Carver, a distinguished eighteenth-century Irish landscape painter, has also been recorded in association with the Dublin pottery.) These barrels clearly demonstrate the fact that Ireland's eighteenth-century potters drew much of their inspiration from continental rather than English ceramics. The form is relatively common in European tin-glazed earthenware, but, as yet, no English delftware barrels of this kind have been recorded.

Delamain Pottery Plate

Irish, Dublin, painter's number '3' under the rim, *c.*1755–70
Delftware, Diam. 26.5
Accession no: HCL 033

For many, the landscape-painted delftwares that were produced in Dublin during the 1750s and 1760s perfectly capture the spirit of Georgian Ireland. Although their designs were clearly based upon continental originals, the Dublin potters rarely achieved quite the same levels of perfection and sophistication. Even in this particularly fine example of Irish delftware, the freehand painting of the hilltop town is rather naïve, closer in character to folk art than many of the fine-quality continental ceramics that the Dublin potters were attempting to imitate.

The pottery of which the plate is made – tin-glazed earthenware or delftware – was also considered in the mid-eighteenth century to be greatly inferior to the perfectly white, translucent porcelains that were then being produced in China, Meissen, Chelsea and elsewhere. Yet this supposedly 'inferior' delftware glaze was much thicker than the thin, clear glaze applied to porcelain. As a result, the painted manganese decoration has sunk into the white tin-glaze and become slightly diffuse, imparting a softness and warmth to the Irish plates that is often lacking among more technically perfect porcelains. This example was made at the World's End Pottery of Delamain & Co.

'More Rum and Sugar' Punchbowl

Irish, Dublin, c.1760–70
Delftware, Diam. 27
Accession no: HM 2001-2

Most Irish delftware styles have been known for many years, but one that originates from Dublin, categorised as 'coarsely painted', was only recognised in 2000 as a result of an archaeological discovery in the USA. This punchbowl, acquired in 2001, was the first intact example of the type to be identified. Some years earlier, in Chesterfield County, Virginia, local historian Mary Ellen Howe noticed building work in progress on the site of an eighteenth-century tavern. Her subsequent investigation there uncovered delftware fragments that are now recognised as the most important assemblage of eighteenth-century Irish ceramics yet discovered in North America.

In one small trench, the remains of 43 delftware punchbowls were found. All had been broken and buried at about the same time. Had a shelf in the tavern collapsed? Or a stack of bowls fallen off a cart? Many fragments bore a typical Dublin painter's number on the base, but the decoration was more 'coarsely painted' and swiftly executed than any other previously known Irish delftware. Six bowls were painted with the 'Three-window House' design that can be seen here and bore the same painter's number '2'. The only significant difference is that this example is inscribed: 'More Rum and Sugar', whereas those from Virginia bear the legend 'One Bowl More Will' or, in modern parlance, 'One for the Road'.

Hors-d'œuvre or Sweetmeat Set

Irish, Dublin, c.1760–70
Delftware, w 22.5
Accession no: HCL 036-041

These sets of serving dishes, usually consisting of five small, interlocking dishes within a larger tray, are comparatively common in eighteenth-century Chinese and English porcelain but more rare in delftware. They probably formed part of a standard dinner service, and they clearly demonstrate how meals, manners and table etiquette became increasingly sophisticated in affluent Irish homes as the eighteenth century progressed. Each individual dish would have been placed on the dinner table to serve portions of sauces, pickles or condiments.

The painted floral design, known as the 'Flower Spray and Ribbon' pattern, was copied precisely from Chinese porcelain of the 1760s. Almost indistinguishable sweetmeat sets were produced in Liverpool delftware at the same time, but when compared in detail the Irish sets are found to have a unique, distinctive form. The presence of a painter's number is another typical Dublin characteristic, and in this case, as the number '2' is present on all six dishes, they were likely to have been decorated by the same individual.

Most marks recorded on Dublin delftware during the 1750s are painters' monograms, and so the presence of the painter's number would suggest that this set was made slightly later, probably during the 1760s.

Delftware Plate

?Irish, Dublin, 1764
Delftware, Diam. 23
Accession no: HCL 034

This charming plate, one of a pair, may have been made as a christening gift to commemorate the birth of Mary Ann Freno in 1764. It is rare to find names and dates on eighteenth-century Irish or English delftware, and even rarer to find the name inscribed in black (achieved by using very intense, dark-purple manganese). Although no other example of this design is recorded, the four floral motifs around the border also occur on one of the most common Dublin delftware patterns, the 'Chinese Flower-bowl' design. The same pattern was also produced in Liverpool, but small details in the flower painting suggest this plate is more likely to have been made in Ireland.

The unusual and distinctive surname, Freno, provides few clues to the plate's origin. It appears to be an anglicised version of the Huguenot surnames Frenot, Fresnau or Freigneaux. The Mary Ann Freno in question may have been descended from one Andrew Freigneaux, who was made a freeman of the Guild of Glovers in Dublin in 1710. The only family listed in Huguenot records with the same Freno spelling, however, seems to have lived in Cornwall during the 1720s.

Water Bottle ('Gugglet') and Wash-basin

?English, London, *c.*1770
Delftware, Diam. (of basin) 27 –
H (of bottle) 23.6
Accession nos: HCL 051 (basin); 052 (bottle)

Delftware water bottles and wash-basins
are not uncommon, but it is rare for the
two pieces of an eighteenth-century
washing set to have survived together.
The everted rim of this basin suggests it
was designed to rest snugly in the circular
aperture on top of a mahogany wash-
stand. Standards of personal hygiene
were not as high in the eighteenth century
as they became later. Men and women
only rarely bathed in tubs, but it was
considered important at least to keep the
hands and face clean, as the British
statesman, orator and man of letters Lord
Chesterfield told his son: 'Nothing looks

more ordinary, vulgar, and illiberal than
dirty hands.'

Two further bottle and basin sets that
survive bear striking resemblance to this
example. One, in Bristol Museum,
England, is finely painted with a similar
chinoiserie scene. Another, at Historic
Deerfield in New England, features an
identical, crinkle-edged basin. All three
sets are attributed to London. It is also
worth noting that this example is
unusually highly fired for delftware; the
bottle particularly resembles tin-glazed
stoneware. One reason that this bottle and
basin remain in so pristine a condition,
therefore, might be that they were
slightly harder and more robust than most

Plate with Border of Irish Harps and Shamrocks

?Irish, Belfast, c.1800–06
Pearlware, Diam. 26
Accession no: HCL 061

This superbly painted pearlware plate is one of a rare group with identical moulded border designs of Irish harps and shamrocks that are tentatively attributed to the Downshire Pottery, Belfast (active c.1787 to 1796 and c.1800 to 1806). A second plate of this type in the Museum features a naively painted stag, while a third, in a private collection in America, is painted with a fancy bird perched among foliage (a 'peafowl' pattern). Although the site of the Downshire Pottery was excavated in 1993, all of the pottery fragments recovered there were found to have been made before 1793.

Very little is known of the pottery's second phase of operation, after 1800, when these plates would have been produced. In recent years, four examples have also been recorded of some related plain white, oval creamware platters with precisely the same 'Harp and Shamrock' border. These were all found in collections around Belfast in the few years since the excavations took place, which lends further weight to the Belfast attribution. To date, fewer than 20 examples of Irish creamware have been identified, and this zebra plate might well be one of the more spectacular surviving examples. Until further evidence is discovered, however, the possibility will always remain that these plates were instead made in England or Scotland, designed specifically for the Irish market.

Tankard

Northern European, ?south
Netherlands, late 16th century
or early 17th
Tin-glazed earthenware, H 23.6
Accession no: MG 076

This handsome tankard is one
of the most enigmatic ceramic
objects in the Museum. The tall,
cylindrical shape, known as a
schnelle, is distinctively northern
European. German stoneware
tankards of similar form were
produced in quantity from
the 1550s, but the generous
proportions of the handle on
this example relate more closely
to Chinese porcelain tankards
produced for the European market
*c.*1600–50. (It is possible that the
turquoise glaze intentionally imitated
green Chinese celadon porcelains.)

Determining where this tankard might
have been made is difficult, as records
from this early period are scant. Tin-glazed
earthenware was certainly produced in
Germany *c.*1530 onwards, but none of the
wares surviving from this time appear to
bear much resemblance to this example.
The closest comparable wares seem to be
the small group of sixteenth-century delftware known as 'Malling' jugs. These were

long considered the earliest English delftware, but recent evidence suggests they
were more likely produced in the southern
Netherlands. Although this tall, *schnelle*
form is not recorded among known
'Malling' jugs, they sometimes exhibit the
same distinctive, monochrome turquoise
glaze. The high quality gilt-copper mounts
on this tankard also appear to be contemporary fittings – the mythical creature on
the thumb-piece, with a lion's head and
dolphin's tail, is a particularly fine detail.

Pair of Tureens

German, Meissen, *c.*1730–40
Porcelain, w 32.6
Accession no: MG 129A+B

True hard-paste porcelain, identical to the porcelains of China and Japan, was first made in Europe by Johannes Böttger at Dresden *c.*1710. With royal patronage, Böttger soon afterwards established the renowned Meissen factory, which was to reign supreme as the foremost European manufacturer of porcelain throughout the eighteenth century. The truly outstanding quality of Meissen wares ensured that they were widely imitated, but, ironically, many of their most sought-after and desirable designs were themselves imitations of Chinese and Japanese originals.

These tureens clearly demonstrate the extent of this oriental influence on early Meissen. The painted decoration, particularly the restrained use of brilliant enamel colours, with large areas of plain, undecorated, white porcelain, precisely replicates seventeenth-century Japanese porcelains decorated in the *Kakiemon* palette. Perhaps the most obvious signs of European influence lie in the shape of the tureens, which copy silver forms, and also in the handles – finely modelled as female faces with feathered headdresses. The bases of these tureens are flat, with the characteristic blue 'Crossed Swords' mark of Meissen painted directly onto unglazed biscuit. One of the tureens also shows a much rarer mark, an X with four dots at the angles. This is the personal mark of one of Meissen's lesser-known figures, an accomplished potter by the name of Schiefer, who was employed there from before 1728 and into the 1730s.

Sweetmeat Dish in the Form of a Hare

Chinese, late Ming dynasty, reign of Tianqi
(1621–27)
Porcelain, L 17.5
Accession no: MG 116B

This small, Chinese porcelain, sweetmeat or food dish on three circular feet was originally intended for the Japanese market, where such dishes are known as *mokozuke*. Found only rarely in the West, these Chinese blue and white (*ko-sometsuke*) dishes were made in sets of five or 10, following local custom, for the specific purpose of serving food during the *kaiseki* meal that accompanied the formal Japanese tea ceremony. The loose, fluid decoration, strongly influenced by Japanese tastes, also demonstrates the spirit of experimentation that prevailed at China's Jingdezhen kilns during the late Ming period.

Painted details have been swiftly rendered with lines, blue wash and – most significantly – a haphazard scattering of blue spots. This last feature, described as *soufflé* (*fukizumi* in Japan), is the earliest instance of an application technique that ultimately developed into the famous 'powder-blue' ground found on late seventeenth-century Chinese porcelain. Around the rim of the dish, many small glaze flakes can also be seen. Known as dry edge (*mushikui* or insect nibbles in Japan), this feature is a characteristic flaw of late Ming porcelain. In Taoist mythology, the hare is said to dwell on the moon, where it ground the ingredients for the Elixir of Immortality. Hares were thus held in special regard as symbols of longevity in both China and Japan.

'Transitional' Period Jar and Cover

Chinese, early Qing dynasty, reign
of Shunzi, *c*.1644–61
Porcelain, H 37
Accession no: DG 106

This jar is a fine example of
'Transitional' porcelain, the
term applied to Chinese wares
dating from *c*.1620 to 1670,
which span the transition
between the Ming dynasty (which
ended in 1644) and the succeeding
Qing dynasty. The painted decoration
has been achieved by combining
underglaze colour (cobalt blue) with
overglaze coloured enamels. During this
early period, only a limited range of
overglaze enamels were known to Chinese
potters, in most cases, as here, being
restricted to green, red, yellow, black and
aubergine. (The palette is often referred to
as *wucai* or 'five-colour' enamels.)

Working in this mixture of underglaze
and overglaze decoration demanded
planning and skill. The cobalt-blue areas
were painted before the jar went into the
kiln for its final, high-temperature firing.
All of the additional colours were added
later using a low-temperature muffle kiln,
but incorporating the underglaze blue
rocks, sky and clothing details into the
final design. The scene of children playing
in a rocky garden with female attendants is
typical of the period – an important
comparable piece is the famous Tyson Jar,
dated 1646, in the Chicago Art Institute,
Illinois. Large, coloured jars of this kind
must have been expensive, exclusive items
in the West – they were not ordered as
standard cargo by the East India Company
and were probably imported privately by
wealthy individuals.

Pair of *Rouleau* or 'Roll Wagon' Vases

Japanese, Arita, late 17th century
Porcelain, H 29
Accession no: MG 104

These unusual vases, which at first glance appear to be Chinese, are in fact rare examples of early Japanese porcelain. (An identical pair is to be found in the collection of Augustus the Strong, preserved at the Porcelain Palace in Dresden.) The palette of enamel colours is particularly unusual for Japanese porcelain, closely imitating Chinese *famille verte* wares. The tall, cylindrical form, known in sevententh-century Europe by its

Dutch nickname 'Roll Wagon' is also a precise copy of Chinese vases produced from *c*.1640 to 1670. Perhaps the most confusing feature is the fact that the base is unglazed and entirely flat, with no footrim. Such bases are rarely recorded among early Japanese wares but are a very common feature on Chinese vases and jars of the same date. Chinese and Japanese potters often copied one another during the seventeenth century in their attempts to satisfy the changing tastes of the European market, but it is rare to find quite this degree of correspondence in the porcelain they produced.

Imari Ware Bowl and Cover

Japanese, Arita, *c.*1680–1700
Porcelain, H 26
Accession no: MG 101

Arita is a small town on Kyushu,
the westernmost island of Japan,
where for centuries some of the
finest Japanese porcelains have
been made. The nearby seaport of
Imari, from which many of these
exotic wares were exported, gave its
name to one particularly distinctive group,
which decorated in a palette of underglaze
blue and overglaze red and gold. This
covered bowl is a textbook example of the
earliest Japanese Imari ware.

Deep bowls with covers of this kind
are commonly referred to as tureens or
(when they have lost their lids) *cachepots*
(Fr. flowerpot holders), but the form
seems to be oriental, and its original
function is in fact unclear. In common
with many Japanese bowls of this period,
the handles seem disproportionately
small and insubstantial, but these are

compensated for here by the very finely
modelled finial in the form of a Buddhist
guardian 'Lion Dog' or 'Shishi'. The silver
rim was added when the bowl arrived in
Europe, perhaps as an additional mark of
quality or simply to disguise rim chips that
would have detracted from its value.
European silver rims, lids, spouts and handles are commonly found on early oriental
porcelain, but this example is unusual in
that it bears the touch mark 'SH' or 'HS'
of an unidentified silversmith.

Pair of Pug Dogs

Chinese, *c.*1745–60, Qing dynasty, reign of
Qianlong (1736–95)
Porcelain, H 25
Accession no: MG 113A+B

Although the pug is native to China, the
design source for this pair of Chinese
canine figures was European. Johann
Joachim Kändler first modelled porcelain
pug dogs at the Meissen factory near
Dresden in 1738, but they proved so
popular that many different versions were
subsequently produced by porcelain and
faience potteries throughout Europe.
These Chinese examples, although more
stilted and stiff than Kändler's originals,
were among the largest pug figures
produced anywhere. Each one was press
moulded; an open, vertical scar on the
chest of one figure clearly shows how the

two moulded halves were joined. The pug
was first popularised in Europe by
William III during the late seventeenth
century (when they were known as 'Dutch
Dogs', or in Germany, *Mops*). Their widespread popularity may also reflect the fact
that the pug came to represent the emblem
of a secret society known as the *Mopsorden*
or 'Order of the Pug'. This pseudo-
masonic fraternity – open to both men
and women – was formed soon after 1738
when the Pope expressly prohibited
Roman Catholics from membership of the
Freemasons, on pain of excommunication.
These figures might therefore have held
hidden significance at the time they were
made, displaying to those who understood
the symbolism that their owner was of
pro-Catholic persuasion and perhaps even
a Freemason.

Puppy and Kitten Figures

Japanese, Arita province, c.1680–1700
(puppy); late 19th century (kitten)
Porcelain, H (of puppy) 17.5; (of kitten) 14.8
Accession no: MG 117A + B

Although these two Japanese porcelain
figures look remarkably similar, they were
in fact made almost two centuries apart.
Some of the earliest documented examples
of Japanese porcelain figures are preserved
at Burghley House, Cambridgeshire. The
collection there, first inventoried in 1688,
includes a pair of puppies that share a
strong affinity with the example here. The
puppy, therefore, appears to be a genuine
and rare seventeenth-century Japanese
porcelain figure. The 'beckoning kitten'
initially seems to be rarer still – cats are
even more scarce in seventeenth-century

Arita porcelain than puppies. Yet small
details in the character of the porcelain,
the enamelling and the modelling reveal
that the kitten is actually nineteenth
century in date. (It is more difficult to tell
whether the figure is simply a late example, made in traditional fashion, or a deliberately deceptive copy.) Ceramic animals
are still produced as folk toys and gifts in
Japan to this day. Cats are believed to
summon good luck and prosperity, and
these figures are often placed by the
entrance of homes and shops. (A raised
left paw is thought to beckon customers; a
raised right one welcomes cash.) Puppies
for their part are associated with good
luck and protection from evil. They are
usually given to newborn baby boys to
keep them safe from harm.

Wine Ewer

Chinese, Qing dynasty, late 18th
or 19th century
Porcelain, H 26.2
Accession no: MG 116d

It is difficult to provide a certain identity
for this work, largely because few
comparable examples appear to have been
recorded. A handwritten note, probably
penned by John Hunt himself in the
1950s, was recently found inside the ewer,
stating that – in the opinion of one
knowledgeable authority of the time – the
ewer was 'definitely eighteenth century
and not later'. Blue-and-white Chinese
porcelain wine ewers were in fact popular
as early as the late Ming dynasty (late
sixteenth century), and aspects of the floral
decoration on this piece do suggest a
deliberate attempt to imitate porcelains of
this period.

Overall, however, the ewer's design, the
costume and hairstyle of the figure, the
flat, rather uniform floral painting and a
distinctively late footrim would all suggest
that the ewer was made long after the

Ming dynasty ended in 1644. The base
appears to be the most reliable dating
characteristic, and using this as our guide
then the ewer may date from the late
eighteenth or (more probably) the
nineteenth century. Even so, this remains
an interesting and rare example of
Chinese porcelain. The design seems so
novel and attractive that it prompts the
question of why so few examples appear
to exist.

Ivory, bone, coral and glass

Drinking Horn

Northern German or
Scandinavian, late
15th century
Horn with silver-gilt mounts,
H 20 × W 24 × D 10
Accession no: CG 033

This drinking horn is typical of those made throughout Europe between the tenth and the seventeenth century. Most northern European versions of the fifteenth century and later have clawed feet and Late Gothic-style ornament. This particular example (one of two in the Museum) is characteristic of the late medieval 'Griffin's Foot' or 'Dragon's Foot' style, in which the feet are separately made and soldered on. The animal horn is banded by silver-gilt mounts with stylised foliage, and the terminal has incised ornamentation of meandering foliage and a brambled knob. The rim, decorated with incised and hatched work, is riveted in place, and bears an inscription that may have been added in the sixteenth century. Its foliated ornament recalls that found on some of the Raeren jugs, which can also be seen in the Museum.

Drinking horns were frequently given as gifts and used as charter horns to seal land and other legal agreements. They are common throughout northern Europe: an Irish version, the fifteenth-century Kavanagh Charter horn, is to be found in the collection of the National Museum of Ireland, Dublin; a Scandinavian example bears the names of the Three Wise Men.

Stained-glass Panel of Angel with a Trumpet

English, *c.*1300
Glass, H 45 × W 28.4
Accession no: CG 042

This panel, and the four others in the Collection, may have come from Bristol Cathedral, a former Augustinian Abbey. Charles Winston, a pioneer of medieval stained-glass studies, recorded the Angel with the Trumpet and fragments of the other Angel musicians during renovations to Bristol Cathedral in 1848. They probably formed part of a band of angel musicians high in the tracery above a scene of the Last Judgement. The style of the figure and the painting of the features suggest that the glass dates from the early phase of the Abbey's construction.

This particular panel depicts an angel in a long white flowing robe, blowing a trumpet. The figure is elongated, the wings green and the hands and feet flesh-coloured. The face, painted directly onto the glass, is oval with wide, staring eyes, a prominent nose that sweeps up to form an eyebrow and stylised hair set close to the head in short curls. The blue background highlights the variations in depth of colour that are typical of early glass, held together in this instance by thin strips of grooved lead.

Figure of Christ the Good Shepherd

Indo-Portuguese,
Goa, 17th century

Elephant ivory,
H 19 × W 6.5

Accession no:
HCM 098

Following the discovery of the route to India round the Cape of Good Hope by the celebrated Portuguese navigator Vasco da Gama, Portuguese settlers established a colony in Goa in 1510. When the Jesuits arrived there as missionaries in 1542, they began to adapt local religious symbols to fit in with Christian iconography. It is possible that they used a specific Indian art motif, one of a young boy on a hill surrounded by images of fountains and sheep, as an aid to their religious teachings.

This particular ivory figure, a representation of Christ the Good Shepherd, is typical of a group of similar figures to be found in many museums around the world. The carved heart on which it sits is decorated with red paint; beneath it two birds, possibly peacocks, drink from a fountain, the symbol of life. The flesh of the peacock was traditionally believed to never decay, and the Church adapted this idea for use as a symbol of the resurrection of Christ. St Catherine, patron of Goa – with her attribute, a book – is carved at the base. There are lambs and two lions couchant on either side of the base. Traces of gilding can be found all over the figure. The branch, adjacent to it, originally belonged to the piece, attached at the back of the carving, with God the Father – the first person of the Trinity – at the top.

Carving of Isis Suckling Horus

Egyptian, ?Alexandria, late 1st–early 2nd
century
Bone, H 8.9 × W 3.2
Accession no: HCM 102

This bone relief carving, representing the
Egyptian goddess Isis suckling her son,
the god Horus, was probably produced in
Alexandria in the late first or early second
century. The image of Isis suckling
Horus remained unchanged in Egypt for
about 2,000 years; it depicted Isis in a
tight tunic and black wig, sitting rigid
and expressionless on a low stool and
supporting Horus stiffly with her left arm
as she offers him her right breast. Her
sacred symbols, two curving horns
surrounding a sun disc, were worn on her
head. The Greeks, under Alexander the
Great, defeated the Egyptians in 332 BC
and 300 years later were themselves
defeated by the Romans. Both regimes
honoured the great Egyptian gods Isis,
Osiris and Horus, but they slowly adapted
the image of the popular goddess from the
stiff Egyptian stance to a Graeco–Roman
model. Her Greek clothes, elaborate
hairstyle, relaxed, graceful posture and
delicate features have been achieved here
in bone, a notoriously fragile material.
A small hole in the top of her head shows
where the sacred symbols, now lost, were
attached with a mortise, making her
instantly recognisable throughout the
Roman Empire.

Love Pair Pendant

European, ?16th century with later
additions
Ivory, gold, emeralds, ruby, enamel,
pearls, H 11 × W 6 × D 0.5
Accession no: T 001

This splendid piece of jewellery consists of
an ivory carving of a nymph and satyr in an
amorous embrace, supported by an ornate
crescent-shaped gold mount, decorated
with enamelled scrolls, three emeralds,
one ruby, three large drop pearls and two
smaller round ones. The ivory shows
traces of paint, yellow on the hair of the
nymph, blue on the cloak and green on the
ground surface. The pendant hangs from
two separate chains, each of 20 round
links, joined at the top by an enamelled
scroll motif with tiny blue stones, a central
cabochon ruby and pendant pearl.
The back has engraved motifs coloured in
green, blue and amber.

The ivory carving may be a copy of a wall
mural found during excavations at
Herculaneum, buried, with Pompeii, by
Vesuvius in AD 79. Many erotic scenes
adorned the interiors of the houses there,
and when rediscovered, they were
concealed on Papal orders. Now pain-
stakingly restored, they are to be found in
the Archaeological Museum, Naples,
where they have a special place in the
Cabbineto Segreto. The ivory may be a
later addition to an otherwise sixteenth-
century base. It would have been worn
either as a neck pendant or sewn high on
a sleeve.

Carved Coral Ring

Italian, setting mid-19th century, stone earlier
Coral and gold, H 4 × W 2.5 × D 2.3
Accession no: T 020

The ring's stone is coral, carved into the three-dimensional head of a man wearing a North African headdress. The coral is worn, and the carving, though competent, is not sharp. It is difficult to date precisely, but it may precede the creation of its setting. The carving might have been either the top of a seal or stick, perhaps from as early as the seventeenth century, or an element in a later bracelet.

Before the early to mid-nineteenth century coral was mostly worn for its amuletic qualities, particularly as a protection against the evil eye, often for infants. It later became popular in jewellery, especially once – with cameos and mosaics – it began to be brought home in quantity from Italy, by travellers as a souvenir. Naples was the centre to which 'noble coral' was brought. This red or rose-red jewellery quality material is found off the coasts of Tunisia, Algeria, Sicily, Corsica and the Italian region of Calabria.

The hoop of the ring seems over delicate compared to the massive stone. It features granulation (decoration with small metal beads, a skill much used in Etruscan work and copied in the mid-nineteenth century), twisted gold wire and applied floral and leaf motifs in coloured gold, mixed with silver, to give a greenish tinge, and with copper, to give a red tone.

Comb with Scenes from the Life of King David and Bathsheba

French, 15th century
Walrus ivory, H 12 × W 16.04
Accession no: HCM 150

John Hunt purchased this comb from the collection of Lord Astor. It is a broad 'H' comb, double-edged and cut with one row of fine and another of coarse teeth, and delicately carved on a hatched background with foliage and flowers. The front central panel depicts three naked dancing females, each holding a draped cloth in her arms. A crowned figure playing a harp sits by a fountain, the symbol of life. On the reverse of the comb the same figure leans over a naked couple lying together. There are two dancing females and a hill and trees in the background. It was fashionable for ivory to be painted, and remnants of paint can be seen on the flowers.

During the Gothic period, combs, mirrors and *gravoires* (hair parters) were included in the *trousse de toilette* (dressing case) of a lady or gentleman. While *peigniers* (comb makers) specialised in the manufacture of combs, artists carved the scenes. Religious imagery appears on those combs intended for matters sacred, such as those for use by the church, for example, during the consecration of a bishop. Those carved with mythological, romantic, hunting or battle scenes were intended for more worldly use, as is this one, depicting as it does an episode from the life of King David and Bathsheba, which is one of the themes commonly used on more secular combs.

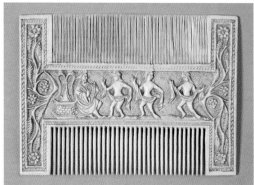

Cylindrical Casket

Siculo-Arabic, late 12th or early 13th century
Ivory, H 11 × W 11 × D 10
Accession no: CG 010

This casket is an example of one made by Arab craftsmen in Sicily during a period of German rule, a time when the cultural influence of Islam was welcome, and from when the term Siculo-Arabic derives. Many such caskets were made with a hipped roof and decorated with semi-precious stones.

The circular shape of this casket is achieved by holding together two half circles of ivory with mounts on one side, a good and practical illustration of the use of the natural shape of the elephant tusk. The lid is made from an ivory disc, its outer rim secured with a bronze mount.

The mounts and feet are uniform in style and contemporary with the casket, and may originally have been gilded. On many such caskets, including a similar one in the Schnütgen-Museum, Cologne, the plate also has a keyhole. This example has none. Inside, it is lined with what appears to be appliquéd felt, probably a later addition, and there are traces of Arabic script where the lining has worn away.

These caskets were made as containers, and the Latin word *custodium* is found on the wooden base. Sometimes attributed to the fourteenth century, on the basis of comparison with similar caskets it is more likely to be late twelfth or early thirteenth century.

Gyldensteen Cross

English, late 12th century
Ivory, H 7.2 × W 5.7
Accession no: BM 001

John Beckwith gives this reliquary cross a date of the late twelfth century. John Hunt purchased it at Sotheby's on Friday 17 March 1961 from the collection of Count Bernstorff Gyldensteen. The catalogue noted that no other ivory cross appears to have been recorded. For some years it was exhibited in the British Museum, London, and was only returned to the Hunt Collection in 1998.

The cross is made in two pieces, which, when put together, form a box in the shape of a crucifix, perhaps to contain a relic of the true cross. It would have been used as a personal devotional piece. On one side the Lamb of God is carved within a quatre-foil, surrounded by the symbols of the four Evangelists: Matthew, John, Luke and Mark. On the other, Christ is shown on the cross with the hand of God (*Dextera Dei*) above him. The hand, emerging from a cloud above Christ's head, was an early representation of the first person of the Trinity. One foot overhangs the frame, and the finely carved loincloth falls below the knee. The eyes are inlaid with either jet or paste. Both sides are decorated with a spiral leaf scroll.

Plaque with Nativity Scenes

Mosan or German, *c*.1100–50
Ivory, H 14.6 × W 10.4
Accession no: CG 005

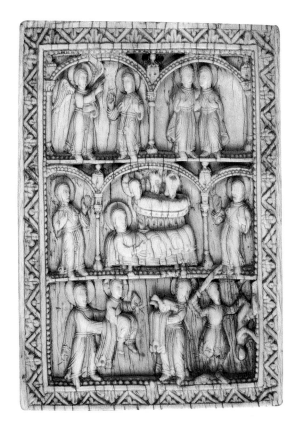

Thin plaques of ivory were often used in the Middle Ages to embellish the covers of books, the ivory forming a centrepiece surrounded by ornamental bands of metalwork. This is the most likely function of this unusual Romanesque-style plaque.

The plaque is carved with narrative scenes in three registers. The top two registers are framed by beaded arches; shortage of space forced the artist to eliminate the arcades and cut off the haloes in the bottom register. The narrative starts with the Annunciation and the Visitation. Then follows the Birth of Christ, witnessed by two mysterious figures sometimes identified as Salome and Joseph; similar figures can be found in at least one German ivory of the period. The bottom register is largely occupied by the presentation of Christ in the Temple, but again the iconography is peculiar, for there is no sign of Simeon, the aged figure who took the infant Jesus in his arms and recognised him as the Messiah. The Massacre of the Innocents at the extreme right is represented by a single soldier about to slaughter an infant.

The sculptor's style is identified by the solidly modelled figures and distinctive sweeps of drapery with parallel folds. Such techniques, combined with other features of the plaque – the beaded arches, the design of the figures and the arrangement of the drapery over the Virgin Mary's bed – may be related to ivories from Germany and the Meuse valley region of western Europe.

Late Renaissance Jug

Italian, late 16th or early 17th century
Glass with gilt base-metal mounts, H 20.7
Accession no: HCL 022

This late Renaissance jug belongs to a
small yet instantly recognisable group of
ornamental vessels, in which the hollow
body is the only section made of glass.
The remainder of the jug – the foot, stem,
handle, pierced strap-mounts – is of gilt
base metal, produced in a separate workshop but presumably to the same design
as that used by the glassmaker when
blowing the glass (usually emerald green
or deep blue).

These vessels were never mounted in
gold or silver gilt, unlike their hardstone
counterparts; their function, therefore,
was decorative. The designer is not known
nor, indeed, has the precise date or place
of the vessels' origin ever been established.
However, a drawing by Giovanni Maggi,
c.1604, now in the Uffizi, Florence,
provides the earliest record of a mounted
glass flask.

The production of this distinctive group
is unlikely to have lasted, even though
several examples (in the form of vases)
were depicted by Neapolitan, Spanish and
Netherlandish artists of the mid- to late
seventeenth century. Other collections
with related examples include the British
Museum, London; the Museo Civico,
Turin; the Veste Coburg collection in
Germany and the Rothschild Collection at
Waddesdon Manor, Buckinghamshire.

Devotional Diptych Panel

French, 14th century
Ivory, H 6.6 × W 4.2 × D 0.6
Accession no: HCM 086

In ancient Rome the inside panels of the diptychs were coated with wax to facilitate inscription and given to friends by consuls to mark their term of office. In later centuries their use changed from the secular to the devotional, and they were decorated with carved biblical and religious scenes. The style of carving on diptychs throughout the Gothic period reflects that used by manuscript illuminators and stone carvers in cathedrals.

Many panel carvers worked with ivory, and Paris was the centre for ivory carving until the fifteenth century when small panel paintings became a popular substitute. This panel is the left half of a pair previously hinged together. The upper register depicts Adam and Eve's banishment from the Garden of Eden by a sword-wielding angel, in which they try to cover their nakedness with fig leaves. The lower register shows the Labours of Life, the results of the Fall, in which Adam digs while Eve spins. To the right, Eve is suffering the pains of childbirth, attended by a physician holding a phial of medicine.

Carving of John the Evangelist

German, 13th century
Ivory, H 11.6
Accession no: HCM 084

This small carving of John the Evangelist was originally part of a crucifixion scene. A small wooden peg to be found in the base of the statue would have fixed it initially to a group, in which it stood with a carving of Mary, mother of Jesus. John, son of Zebedee and one of the favoured Apostles, holds a palm that, it is said, he received from the Virgin on her deathbed. Traditionally believed to have written the fourth Gospel of the New Testament and the Apocalypse, he is sometimes shown holding a book, a symbol of his writings.

These groups were devotional objects and influenced by other pieces made of stone and wood. The Crucifixion was frequently represented in a range of materials, which includes an eleventh-century mosaic to be found in the monastery church at Daphne, Greece. There are traces of paint on this carving, but it is not clear whether this is original: conservators working on polychromed ivories often find that overpainting occurred in the seventeenth and eighteenth centuries. In ancient times ivory was valued on a par with gold, and being easy to carve, it maintained its appeal to craftsmen throughout the centuries.

Carving of St Thomas à Becket

?English, 12th century
Walrus ivory, H 8.5 × W 2.89
Accession no: MG 027

This carved ivory piece depicts a scene from the life of St Thomas à Becket. The group is carved from walrus ivory, more readily available in northern regions than elephant ivory. It shows four knights, the number involved in the murder in 1170 of Becket in Canterbury Cathedral, following a dispute with Henry II. One knight holds an axe with which to break down the door of the Cathedral. There are two tonsured figures in the centre; the hole between them may have held a cross. The three figures to the front include an archbishop (or bishop), holding a staff, and two clergymen.

News of Becket's murder created shock waves as it spread across Europe. Canonised by Pope Alexander III by 1173, the cult that grew up around him led to the manufacture of mementoes for pilgrims to Canterbury. These were made in a variety of materials and forms, including ivory and bronze, tapestry and painting.

The Beverley Crosier

Anglo-Norman, late 11th century
Walrus ivory, H 9.8, w 6.4 (volute)
Accession no: BM 002

This carving of a crosier head depicts St John of Beverley performing a healing miracle. It is said that he taught and ordained the Venerable Bede, patron saint of scholars, who recorded how St John of Beverley cured a dumb boy in AD 685. This story relates to accounts of a miracle performed by SS Peter and John, in which they healed a cripple in the temple.

Professor Francis Wormald identifies the inscription on the crosier head as relating to St John of Beverley. He also suggests that the scene on the reverse relates to the Harrowing of Hell. There are leaf scrolls containing animals and an inscription on the stem with evidence of a repair on the volute.

St John of Beverley was Archbishop of York from 705 to 717 and died in 721. He was canonised in 1037. A later bishop of York commissioned a biography in the 1060s, and it is possible that the crosier was requested at the same time. The style of carving is similar to that of late eleventh-century Anglo-Norman book illumination.

Cannock Tait & Co. Decanter

?English, mid-19th century
Glass, H 14.5
Accession no: HCL 026

This small glass decanter has an everted
flat rim, three ribs on the neck and a
spherical stopper that may or may not be
the original. It bears the name of Cannock
Tait & Co., Limerick, in gold lettering.

This decanter is significant more for its
link to the commercial life of Limerick
than as an example of fine or individual
craftsmanship. Cannock Tait & Co. was
originally established in 1850 by John
Arnott and George Cannock, with Peter
Tait, a self-made entrepreneur, who served
three terms as Mayor of Limerick, and
Michael Cleary, who established Cleary's
in Dublin, subsequent shareholders.

The store had an impressive trading
history, employing up to 300 people at its
peak. A major reconstruction in 1858 gave
it an impressive façade, and the addition
in 1888 of a clock tower, including a
Westminster five-bell chime clock,
established the shop as a city landmark.
The store had a reputation for quality
products, reflected in its participation at
the 1882 National Exhibition, Dublin, with
exhibits of furniture, upholstery and
Limerick lace. Following a number of
resisted takeover bids in the 1960s, the
firm of Winston's gained a controlling
share. The flagship premises were sold in
1980 to the Penney's chain with
Cannock's moving to the Winston
premises in William Street. Cannock's
ceased trading and went into liquidation
in 1984.

Pair of *Zwishengoldglas* Beakers

German, *c.*1730
Glass, H 8 × w 7.5; H 8 × w 6.4
Accession no: DG 078; 077

Gold sandwich-glass or *zwishengoldglas* vessels have decorated gold foil sealed between two layers of glass, one of which may be coloured or lacquered. Archaeologists digging at Canosa, in Italy, found such vessels dating from the third century BC. The *fondi d'oro* of Roman glass were gold sandwich-glass medallions decorated with portraits, or religious, mythological or topical themes and inserted into the base of shallow bowls or dishes. The art was revived in Bohemia in the early eighteenth century. It demanded great expertise, and the beakers and goblets created there were beautiful and valuable objects, fit for nobility.

DG 078 is a flared and facetted *zwishengoldglas* beaker with a continuous gilt frieze of a hunting scene between two borders of acanthus leaves. Three horsemen and four attendants on foot with hounds are holding a stag and doe at bay. Two hounds are savaging a hare on the red base medallion.

DG 077 is a flared beaker engraved with diamond point above a *zwishengoldglas* border of acanthus leaves. A coronet with five leaves and five jewels is represented above a monogram with the letters 'CK', all surrounded by scrolls, swags, foliage and a pair of eagles. The reverse, with further foliate design, bears an inscription in German extolling true friendship. On a ruby-coloured base, in the *zwishengoldglas* technique, a motto surrounds two flaming hearts, one of them winged. This is a friendship glass for a count.

Leopard's Head Ornament

Court of Benin, Edo,
15th–19th century
Ivory with lead inlay,
H 18.5 × W 10 × D 4.4
Accession no: JB 008

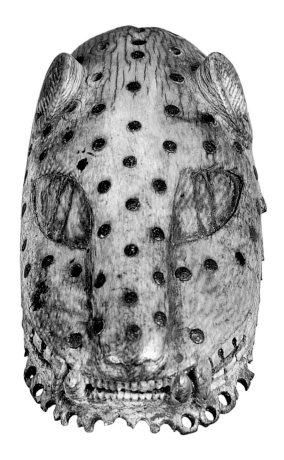

This ivory and lead leopard's head is an Edo ceremonial costume attachment from the royal court of Benin, now incorporated into the modern republic of Nigeria. Edo is the principal tribe of the ancient kingdom of Benin, and the Oba is regarded as its divine monarch. The art of Benin, a royal art to honour the Oba and his ancestors, is predominantly comprised of work in cast brass and carved ivory.

This oval attachment is in elephant ivory, with inlaid lead representing the leopard's spots. The piece is framed at the base by an ornamental flange of concentric circles. The slanted eyes, overlapping fangs and foliate-pattern ears are characteristic of Edo leopard carvings. This particular costume attachment is a hip ornament, usually worn singly over the left hip to adorn the closure of a sarong. While bronze hip ornaments are worn by senior chiefs, those in ivory are the sole prerogative of the Oba.

It is assumed that this ornament formed part of the vast quantity of brass and ivory carvings that were stolen from the royal palace during a punitive expedition to Benin in 1897, and which represented the first sizeable collection of African art to which Europeans were exposed. The objects were subsequently sold by auction in Britain to pay for the expedition. This attachment was among a group of approximately 200 Benin artworks that were purchased by General Augustus Pitt-Rivers.

Metal

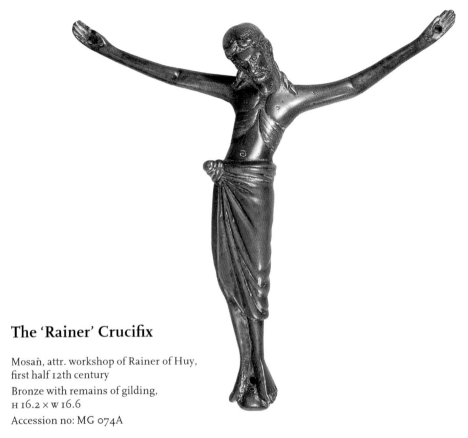

The 'Rainer' Crucifix

Mosân, attr. workshop of Rainer of Huy,
first half 12th century
Bronze with remains of gilding,
H 16.2 × W 16.6
Accession no: MG 074A

This crucifix is attributed to the workshop of Rainer of Huy, an outstanding craftsman, who was active in the early twelfth century in the Meuse valley region (now southern Belgium). Avoiding the linear patterns and geometrical forms generally associated with Romanesque art, Rainer adopted a more classical approach. His name is linked to a spectacular font at Liège, where the draped figures are distinguished by smooth, flowing folds, gracefully wrapped around the limbs.

While there is no certainty that this crucifix was made by Rainer, there is no doubting the influence of his style.

Romanesque crucifixes have been classified according to the manner of the loincloth. This particular crucifix has one of the standard arrangements, with the loincloth knotted beside the right hip, and long diagonal folds stretching across the front. With its elongated proportions, the figure conveys an unusual degree of emotional expression: the head is bent quite sharply and the body sways in a manner that foreshadows the crucifixes of the Gothic era. This is very much an image of the suffering Christ, *Christus patiens*, an impression heightened by the closed eyes.

The 'Red Abbey' Crucifix

?Irish, late 12th or early 13th century
Bronze, H 22
Accession no: HCM 050

There are at least 15 Irish crucifix figures
that survive from the Romanesque period,
and, although badly damaged, the so-
called 'Red Abbey' figure is one of the
finest in quality. The pointed chin, ovoid
eyes and protruding ears all have their
parallels in an Irish context, not least in
the series of bronze figures attached to
St Manchan's shrine at Boher in County
Offaly. More remarkable is the rounded
modelling of the thighs, with a series of
curved folds, which help to accentuate
Christ's physique. The central V-shape
fold was probably copied from English
crucifixes, following the type to which the
so-called 'Pugin' crucifix belongs. The
most unusual feature of the 'Red Abbey'
figure is the series of tiny folds between
the thighs.

A crucifix in the Historical Museum,
Stockholm, thought to be of Scandinavian
provenance, provides some parallels in the
treatment of the loincloth. The simple
flat-top crown occurs on a number of Irish
examples, the crown emphasising the
notion of Christ triumphant, victorious
over death. In this example the feet point
slightly outwards and are nailed separately
to the background cross. Although the
exact circumstances of the find are
unclear, 'Red Abbey' is probably a
reference to Abbeyderg, an Augustinian
priory, founded in County Longford in
1217, somewhat later than the likely date
of the crucifix figure.

The 'Pugin' Crucifix

?English, ?12th century
Bronze, with traces of gilding,
H 18.5 × W 16.5
Accession no: BM 009

Although Christian believers now take the image of the crucifixion for granted, it was not widespread in medieval art until the Romanesque period, when a demand developed for small crucifixes to serve as processional and altar crosses. Before the eleventh century, crosses were not normally placed on the altar; it has been suggested that debates over transubstantiation encouraged churchmen to introduce only those displaying the body of Christ, providing a reminder of the real presence in the bread and wine of the Eucharist.

This example has a distinctive loincloth, with a V-shape fold like an apron in the centre, a specific type linked to English work on the basis of parallels in Anglo-Saxon manuscripts. Although the rigid body and the symmetrical flap of the loincloth reflects the delight in clear geometrical shapes favoured by Romanesque artists, the drapery is treated with some freedom, falling well below knee level at the back. It has a special relevance for Ireland since a crucifix of this type served as a model for the stone sculptor who carved the head of the twelfth-century market cross at Tuam, County Galway.

In later life the crucifix had a distinguished career. It was once owned by the distinguished English architect Augustus Pugin (1812–52), whose passion for the art of the Middle Ages helped to ensure the success of the Gothic Revival.

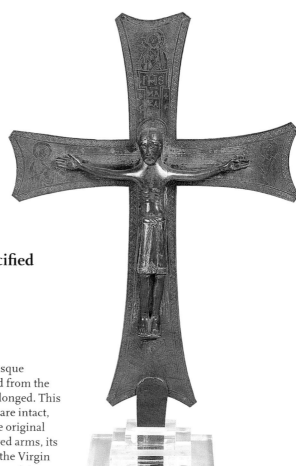

Altar Cross with Crucified Christ

Italian, ?12th century
Gilded bronze, H 34.6 × W 25.5
Accession no: HCM 052

A high proportion of Romanesque crucifixes have been separated from the crosses to which they once belonged. This example, where the two parts are intact, gives a good impression of the original effect. The cross itself has flared arms, its surface thinly engraved, with the Virgin Mary and St John on the arms and the *Majestas Domini* above. A halo on the cross neatly coincides with Christ's head, and immediately above is a *titulus*, referring to Jesus of Nazareth.

The cast figure of Christ is quite symmetrical, the short loincloth having a central fold and knot; further folds are delicately incised on the bronze. Christ's eyes are wide open, staring straight ahead, as if to emphasise his victory over death. His waist is narrow, and the curves of the upper body are gently echoed in the curves of the outstretched arms. One rare detail is the way in which the left thumb is folded against the palm, whereas the right thumb is not.

There is an almost identical altar cross (complete with contrasting thumbs) in Bonn, Germany, and it may be that both were made at the same workshop in central Italy. On the back there is a delicately engraved crucifixion, this time with the head of Christ sagging in death, a contrast to the victorious image on the front. It is accompanied by the symbols of the evangelists. Now difficult to see, the incised drawings on the back were executed in an expressive Romanesque style.

Horse Aquamanile

German, Nuremberg, 15th century
Cast brass, H 27.5 × L 26 × W 8
Accession no: CG 073

The Latin term *aquamanile* is conventionally applied to vessels from which water was poured for hand washing in both domestic and liturgical contexts; it referred originally to the basin into which water was poured. Aquamaniles can be earthenware or metal and variously take the form of animals, birds, equestrian figures and mythical creatures. Handles and spouts are the subject of elaboration.

This horse aquamanile is relatively naturalistic, although a small dragon forms the handle and holds the reins. Water was poured in through a lidded opening in the head; it was tapped at the breast through a beast-head spout that could be closed by a quarter turn. The piece was cast by the lost-wax process, in which the hollow interior is created by suspending a clay core within the mould. This was achieved using short brass rods that were incorporated in the finished casting; they remain visible as small circles of differential coloration. The handle and reins were made separately and attached by soldering, likewise the spigot that holds the spout. Aquamaniles of this type and quality were produced for wealthy patrons in the Bavarian city of Nuremberg. A comparable horse aquamanile is in the Bayerisches Nationalmuseum, Munich. No such vessel is known from medieval Ireland, although metal tableware was imported from the Continent, and two lion aquamaniles have been found in Scotland.

Selection of Axe heads

Flat Axe

Irish, Co. Limerick, final Neolithic/Early Bronze Age
Copper, L 12.5
Accession no: HCA 213

Flat Axe

Irish, Co. Down, Early Bronze Age
Bronze, L 15.3
Accession no: HCA 224

Developed Flat Axe

?Irish, Early Bronze Age
Bronze, L 13.9
Accession no: HCA 228

Developed Flat Axe

Irish, Early/Middle Bronze Age
Bronze, L 13
Accession no: HCA 237

Palstave

Middle Bronze Age
Bronze, L 15.7
Accession no: HCA 266

Socketed Axe

Irish, Co. Armagh, Late Bronze Age
Bronze, L 6.8
Accession no: HCA 287

Small Socketed Axe

Irish, Late Bronze Age
Bronze, L 3.9
Accession no: HCA 300

Copper axes cast in one-piece moulds were the most common metal artefacts in the earliest stages of metal use. These very early metal axes are simple flat shapes, which were hafted, in the same manner as stone axes, by slotting the axe head into a perforated wooden handle. Bronze axes followed, and throughout the Bronze Age axe types were developed that required ever more sophisticated metalworking skills and increasingly effective hafting techniques.

HCA 228 has very slight flanges along its edges, while those on HCA 237 are more pronounced with a transverse stop-ridge between the flanges. These developments show that axes were now hafted in the forked end of an angled wooden shaft rather than via the earlier perforated handles. Further development is seen with the blending together of the flanges and stop-ridge to produce the palstave-type axe and finally the creation of the socketed variety. The more developed axes would have been cast using two-piece moulds, or clay moulds and cores for hollow casting.

Ball-type Brooch

Irish, ?late 9th or early 10th century
Silver, L 15.1
Accession no: HCA 508

This is an example of a ball-type
penannular brooch, which would have
functioned as a dress or cloak fastener.
The type originated in the native Irish
tradition during the second half of the
ninth century. Its fabrication in silver was
made possible for the first time by the
introduction of large quantities of this
precious metal into Ireland by the
Vikings. Early examples of ball-type
brooches, such as this one, exhibit solid
globular terminals with criss-cross
brambled decoration and are consequently
often referred to as a thistle brooch.
They occur quite commonly as single
finds in Ireland, particularly in the
midlands and the south, such as the one
that was found with the famous chalice at
Ardagh, County Limerick.

Scandinavians who had travelled to
Ireland used these brooches and took
examples home with them, and by the
tenth century a variant type (with large
hollow-cast terminals) was being
produced in Scandinavia as well as in
settlements in the Irish Sea region.
Examples of this and of further variant
types have been found in Ireland and
Scandinavia, as well as in Britain and
Russia. It has been suggested, presumably
on the basis of its small size, that this
brooch is a nineteenth-century repro-
duction. However, the details of its
manufacture and the slightly misshapen
state of its pin do not support such
speculation.

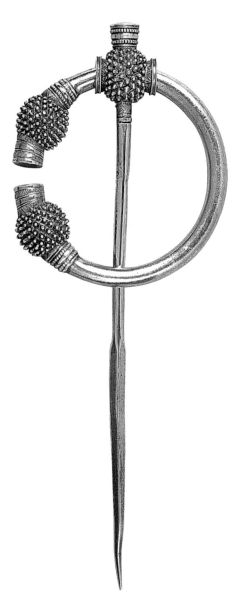

Beaked Flagon
(*Oenochoē*)

Etruscan, 5th century BC
Bronze, H 26 × W 13
Accession no: MG 015

This beaked flagon of beaten bronze
was found somewhere in eastern
France and was acquired from the Ball
Collection in St Alban's, Hertfordshire.
Standing on a slightly splayed base, the
body rises to a tall shoulder, where it
narrows before sloping steeply upward
on one side to the pouring mouth. The
separately cast handle has a terminal at
the lower end, decorated with a palmette,
S-spirals and other shapes, while, above, it
forks before ending in two animal heads.

John Hunt acquired this flagon because
he wrongly believed it to be Celtic – but his
misunderstanding was not too wide of the
mark. Many such vessels (Gr. *oenochoē*)
were manufactured from the late sixth
century BC onwards in Etruria, north of
Rome, and enterprising merchants
brought them up the Rhone valley or
across the Alps. They were placed in Celtic
princely graves, particularly in the
Rhineland, although their central
European distribution stretches widely

from the Marne to Bohemia. By a
fortunate coincidence, the Hunt Museum
also has the only example presumed to
have reached England in antiquity. The
flagons were delivered along with other
Etruscan bronze products, such as buckets
and tripods, for use in feasts of wine,
traces of which are found inside some
flagons. A wine-filled *oenochoē* in a grave
suggests a treasured possession, one
designed to make a prince happy in the
next world.

Chasse

French, late 13th century
Bronze gilt, H 11 × W 15.4 × D 5.3 cm
Accession no: HCM 081

Though without the usual enamel, this house-shaped casket is similar to many of those produced in Limoges in the twelfth and thirteenth centuries. Instead of enamel decoration, the designs are incised into the metal, covering the front, back, roof and both gables. The design consists of a series of roundels, each containing an angel in a different pose, looking to the right or left, up or down. There are three on the front, three on the back and three on each side of the roof. Each gable has one angel in a roundel and another under the eaves.

The engraving is characterised by an emphasis on line: the expression of each angel differs slightly, the loose folds of their robes and their tresses delineated clearly. Simple tendrils of foliage separate the roundels from each other. Ten decorative keyhole shapes pierce the roof ridge. A tapering short column with a knob rises from the centre, while curved knob columns extend over the gables. Each leg is formed by two lengths of metal meeting at right angles, which bend outwards to form two rounded feet at the corners. The legs are covered with simple hatched decoration. The original lock has its key, its handle cusped and trifoliate. The casket was probably used as a reliquary, or for keeping valuables; each would be well guarded by the 16 angels.

A Selection of Spearheads

Early Socketed Spearhead

Early Bronze Age
Bronze, L 13.2
Accession no: HCA 360

Kite-shaped Spearhead

?Irish, Middle/Late Bronze Age
Bronze, L 8.2
Accession no: HCA 333

Kite-shaped Spearhead

?Irish, Middle/Late Bronze Age
Bronze, L 12
Accession no: HCA 334

Basal-looped Spearhead

?Irish, Middle/Late Bronze Age
Bronze, L 9.4
Accession no: HCA 332

Spearhead with Lunate Openings in Blade

Late Bronze Age
Bronze, L 29.6
Accession no: HCA 335

Leaf-shaped Spearhead

Co. Antrim, Late Bronze Age
Bronze, L 21
Accession no: HCA 345

Bronze spearheads were not manu-factured until several centuries after the introduction of metal. The earliest were tanged blades, which probably developed out of contemporary daggers. These were followed by socketed spearheads, where the socket provided a more reliable bond with the wooden spear shaft. In earlier socketed spearheads the socket did not extend far beyond the base of the blade, while on later examples it extends along almost the entire length of the blade. Like the progression from a tang to a socket, the extension of the socket was a techno-logical advance that produced a stronger weapon.

The two large spearheads on the far right (HCA 335 and 345) are representative of forms that were in contemporary use. The largest example is a very showy piece, and it was perhaps valued as much for display as function. The simpler leaf-shaped example on the right (HCA 345) was probably a more utilitarian weapon.

Cashel Bell

Irish, 9th century
Cast bronze, H 30.2 × W 22.4 × D 21.2
Accession no: HCA 617

Handbells are emblematic of the early
insular Church. They are numerous in
Ireland and well represented in Scotland
and Wales. Two categories are recognised,
those made of sheet iron coated with
bronze and those made wholly of cast
bronze. All are quadrangular and provided
with a clapper. The two classes were used
interchangeably, being rung by hand to
mark the canonical hours, to punctuate the
liturgy and to exorcise or ward off evil.
Although bells may have been in use from
the fifth century, most probably date from
between the eighth century and the tenth.
Handbells came to be associated with
individuals and were preserved as relics
of the saints. In the eleventh and
twelfth centuries some iron bells were
enshrined. Handbells vary in size, and
those of bronze are prone to formal
variation.

The Cashel Bell, which is among
the biggest and finest examples, is
further distinguished by a decorative
scheme of engraved ringed crosses
and key patterns. Bells from
Lough Lene, County Westmeath,
and from Bangor, County Down,
are comparable in size and form,
and similarly decorated; all
three may have been made by
the same hand. The Cashel Bell
was found in 1849, but neither
the exact find spot nor the
circumstance of its discovery
was recorded. Vestiges of the
original handle are shown in an
early illustration; the present
handle (which is a little too high)
is a twentieth-century replacement.

Bronze Figure of a Man

European, undated
Bronze, H 8
Accession no: MG 139/024

This unusual and enigmatic work is cast in
bronze. A hole in the sole of each foot
allows it to be attached to a stand or
support, though these holes may be
modern. File marks are visible in many
places, particularly on the hands, which
are sharp featured and fresh looking and
may have been over-cleaned at some stage.
Parallels could be cited across a spectrum
of cultures and periods. The object, if
European, is probably pre-medieval,
though we can only guess as to date,
provenance and function.

The man is shown naked with his hands
and spiky fingers stretched out by his side.
The hips are prominent and the waist is
narrow. The prominent nipples and eyes,
and the general shape of the body recall
some Celtic bronzes of acrobats or figures
on cult vehicles, brooches and statuettes of
various sorts from the late Hallstatt and
early La Tène periods. The absence of ears
is unusual, and the helmet-like head and
the moustache, if such it is, as well as
the general shape of the mouth are
reminiscent of Danish Bronze Age
depictions of various gods. The stretched
triangles above the upper lip also recall
the drooping moustaches of some Viking
sculptures in wood and bronze.

The Cashel Pyx

Irish, mid-18th century
Silver or parcel gilt, D 7.5
Accession no: HCM 125

A pyx is a circular lidded box, in use
from antiquity, and in Christian times
used by the cleric to carry communion
bread to the sick. Often made of silver
or silver gilt, the Cashel pyx is of
parcel gilt. It has a large crucifixion
scene on the front with some
hatching on either side, which gives it
a rough appearance, like bark. The
significance of this is twofold: Christ's
cross was made from a tree, and it was
a tree, furthermore, a fruit tree in the
Garden of Eden, that caused the Fall,
the Fall that Christ redeemed by dying
on a cross. The inscription '*In Cruce
Pendentem Te Iesu Adoro Te*' (Jesus
hanging on the cross I adore you) is to
be seen around the circumference of
the cross, with the dedication 'INRI'
(Jesus of Nazareth King of the Jews)
above it. The inscription on the left is
'*Fran Sall me fieri fecit*' (Franciscan Sall
had me made) and the abbreviated
engraving on the right, '*Pro Tu Conu
Te St Franc Cass I*', is probably a reference to the conventual or high-class
Franciscans. On the obverse, more
crudely worked, is a cross with the
capitals 'IHS', a red heart with three
nails, symbols of the passion.
There is a rope-like surround, a
locking device below and a hanging
ring on top.

Dekadrachma of Syracuse

?Late 5th or early 4th century BC
Silver in a golden frame, H 4.5 × W 4 × D 0.5
Accession no: MG 034

The Greek city of Syracuse produced some of the finest coins of antiquity. Several of the die engravers were so distinguished that their names appear on the coins, though not on this particular example. The main commercial coin of Syracuse was the Tetradrachm or four-drachma piece. This ten-drachma coin is a special minting and may celebrate the victory of the Syracusans over the Athenians in 413 BC or over the Carthaginians in 405 BC. The reverse depicts the nymph Arethusa, presiding deity of the city's chief spring, surrounded by Dolphins (she had come underwater from Greece and her spring was on the shore). The obverse shows a chariot with galloping horses. A Victory is placing a wreath on the head of the charioteer.

This traditional design, modified in the late fifth century to give added movement to the horses, is an expression of the aristocratic nature of the Syracuse government with its depiction of chariot racing, the sport of the rich: Gelon, ruler of Syracuse, had won an Olympic victory in 485 BC. The cuirass, helmet and greaves, below, symbolise military victory. The frame, which probably belongs to the Middle Ages, carries a quotation from St Matthew, '*Quia precium sanguinis est*' (Because it is the price of blood), indicating that it was thought to be one of the 30 pieces of silver given for Christ's betrayal.

Hanging Bowl Escutcheon Disc

Irish/English, 7th century
Bronze with champlevé enamel, Diam. 5
Accession no: MG 040

This small, slightly concave, bronze disc,
formerly in the Londesborough Collection,
still shows traces of red and blue enamel
between the raised lines that form a
central triskele, which unwinds outwards
into three spirals and ends in the trumpet
pattern. Full of life and motion, this design
belongs to the ultimate phase of Celtic
metalwork of La Tène type that decorated
objects in the seventh century, found in
Britain and Ireland. Placed on metal
mounts, such discs ornamented the
escutcheons of bronze bowls, and helped
to suspend them by chain from a stand
or ceiling.

The exact purpose of the bowls has
never been clarified, though one
suggestion is that they functioned as
church lamps. Yet, while the disc's design
finds its closest parallels in Irish metalwork, almost all similar escutcheon discs
have been found attached to bowls that
came from Saxon burials in southern
England.

This example may have originated there,
thus creating an unsolved problem as to
whether they were products of the Irish
Church or of workshops continuing older
Celtic metalworking traditions in a pagan
milieu in Britain. Wherever this disc was
made, it must have been detached from
its original bowl mount and given a
secondary use as a pendant – as indicated
by the crude hole just inside the rim,
which jars in comparison with the design
as originally conceived.

Liturgical 'Heel' Spoon

German, Augsburg, 1618
Silver, L 14.1, w (of bowl) 6
Accession no: HCM 133

This heel spoon is so-called because it can stand upright by means of a triangular-shaped platform at the junction of the stem and bowl. The purpose of the device was to allow the celebrant of the mass to grasp it easily and then convey water into the wine in the chalice. On the front of the bowl in flat chasing is a crucifixion scene with a skull and crossbones at the foot of the cross. Inscribed on the finial of the handle is the date '1618' and over this the dedication 'IS', probably an abbreviation for Jesu Saviour. Where the stem and bowl are joined at the back is a very small impressed area, bearing the town mark of Augsburg, the most important gold-smithing centre in Germany in the seventeenth century. On the back of the heel is a design resembling a palm branch, and on the back of the bowl a leafy and floral flat-chased design.

Figure of Horus

Egyptian, Late Period (664–332 BC)
Bronze, H 19 × W 12 × D 8
Accession no: MG 006

This bronze statuette is of a standing falcon, the form in which the Egyptian god Horus was typically depicted. The eye sockets have been left hollow to allow for an inlay of precious stone or metal. The surface of the figure displays a type of decay very typical of ancient bronzes: the piece would originally have been highly polished and possibly overlaid with precious metal. Horus, the son of Osiris and Isis, was primarily a sky god, though he often took on solar associations, particularly when merged with the sun god Ra. The deity was intimately associated with Pharaoh, who was thought to be the living incarnation of Horus during his reign, before uniting with Osiris, the god of the underworld, after death. The falcon form conveyed notions of power, supremacy and inhabiting the heavenly sky.

From the seventh century BC a vast number of bronze figures of deities were produced in Egypt. Few are properly provenanced, and more precise dating remains difficult. However, continuing excavations reveal that these figures were dedicated as votives at temple sites, including chapels above the galleries that contained sacred animal burials. Subterranean galleries packed with mummified falcons have been found at sites such as Saqqara. Pilgrims could purchase and then dedicate a mummified animal, or a bronze figure of the god, invoking a long life, a child or a good burial. Other examples of bronze figures come from temple furniture, particularly the sacred barques used to transport the image of the god during festival processions.

Midleton Mace

Irish, 18th century
Silver, H 80
Accession no: HCL 085

Derived from weapons carried by royal
bodyguards in England and France in the
medieval period, most civic maces in
Britain and Ireland date from the period
following the Restoration in 1660. King
Charles II, lacking money, sometimes
bought political support by granting
honours and charters. The Corporation of
Midleton in County Cork was established
by a charter of 1670. Midleton was a
pocket-borough of the Brodrick family,
who thus had patronage of two seats in the
Irish House of Commons until 1800.

This mace is of classic Queen Anne
design, having a plain shaft, three knops
and a plain head topped by a crown. The
only other decoration is the engraved
armorial of the Brodricks, an oval shield
set in scrollwork, derived from heraldic
mantling, surmounted by their crest.
The mace bears neither hallmark (a trait of
Irish provincial silver) nor maker's mark.
Its resemblance to the Bandon Mace in the
National Museum of Ireland, Dublin,
suggests that it came from the workshop
of Robert Goble of Cork. The mace may
have been commissioned by Thomas
Brodrick (*d.* 1730) or his younger brother,
Alan, who became Lord Chancellor of
Ireland in 1714, was created a baron in 1715
and first viscount Midleton in 1717.
He died in 1728. The Corporation of
Midleton was abolished in 1840, and all
its real and moveable property reverted to
Lord Midleton.

Communion Cup

Irish, Samuel Wilder, 1696–8
Silver, H 22.8 × Diam. 8.9 (cup)/ 9.8 (foot)
Accession no: HCM 117

The plainness of this silver communion cup is typical of the Church of Ireland plate of its period and a direct result of the Reformation when, in England and subsequently in Ireland, ornate chalices were converted into 'fair and comely cups'. The tradition of more ornate chalices continued in the Roman Catholic Church. This example has a large beaker-style bowl with an everted rim that would have facilitated the distribution of wine to the congregation. The conical stem has a flattened hemispherical knop above a spreading and moulded circular foot.

Most Church of Ireland plates of this period were inscribed with the name of the donor. Here it reads: 'The Gift of the Right Honourable Anne Countess of Tyrone to the Church of Mothell 1697'. Anne's father was Andrew Rickards of Danganspidogue, County Kilkenny. In 1693 she married James Power, third earl of Tyrone, and their only child and heiress, Catherine, married Sir Marcus Beresford, who became successively Viscount and Earl of Tyrone. Their eldest son became the first Marquis of Waterford. The maker's mark 'SW' for Samuel Wilder, a Dublin silversmith, the harp crowned and the date letter 'L' for 1696–8 are shown clearly on the cup. This is one of three known pieces made in the seventeenth century by Samuel Wilder.

Neck-ring

Viking, 10th–11th century
Silver, Diam. 17.5
Accession no: HCA 452

This neck-ring is twisted from pairs of silver rods and features solid, dome-shaped terminals. Though these are of unusual form, in other respects the object is typical of various other Viking-age neck-rings. Several hundred silver neck-rings of this date are on record. Most are from Scandinavia itself. A number of examples, however, are from Ireland and Britain (particularly Scotland). In many instances the neck-rings occur in hoards – deposits of precious metal deliberately concealed with the intention of later recovery.

The more elaborate may have served primarily as status objects, though there is evidence that some were manufactured for the storage of silver in the bullion economies of the Viking world. These would have been weighed during economic transactions, when they were sometimes reduced to the form of 'hack silver' (cut-up fragments of ornaments or ingots) for commercial convenience. Silver ornaments also acquired nicks and pecks, a characteristic Scandinavian method of assessing the quality of the silver and of testing for plated forgeries. One of the rods near the centre of the hoop on this neck-ring exhibits one such nick.

Pendant Reliquary Cross

Spanish/English, *c.*1510
Gold, enamel, pearl, ruby, H 16.5 × W 7
Accession no: CG 085

This reliquary cross shows intricate filigree goldwork of geometric flower design. The extremities are trifoliate, each with a large pearl embedded in its centre, while four more pearls decorate the inner corners of the cross. The outer rim carries four lines written in gold, with some enamel still visible, from the Latin hymn, *Vexilla Regis*, written *c.* AD 600 in praise of the Cross and suggesting that the reliquary may once have held a portion of it. White enamel covers the body of Christ, a small ruby indicating the spear wound. The hair, beard and perizonium remain gold.

An open-work globe with two rings surmounts the cross, allowing it to be worn. The reverse side of the cross has similar gold filigree, with five enamelled circular panels showing the Evangelists and the Lamb of God. Within, a sealed paper packet, with the words '*ex sanguine Thomae Cant. archiepis opi*', indicates that it may also have contained a relic of St Thomas à Becket, who was killed in his cathedral at Canterbury in 1170. Relics were worn as a protection against evil, and there are several portraits of Spanish Infantas or royal children, wearing reliquary crosses and other amulets.

Pomander or *Memento Mori* Skull

?English, 1679
Gold, H 1.9 × D 2.7
Accession no: MG 086

This pomander or *memento mori* is a highly polished skull, skilfully hammered out of a solid piece of gold. It has deeply sunken eye sockets and protruding cheekbones. There is a space between the upper and the lower teeth. The skull can be opened using the clasp at the top, with the back and the front joined together by a hinge. A thin sheet of polished gold, engraved with the inscription 'Man proposes but God disposes', separates the back and front of the skull. This quotation comes from the influential devotional work *The Imitation of Christ* (*c.*1415–24) by the religious writer Thomas à Kempis (1380–1471). There are four compartments in the back for perfume or fragrant herbs. The maker is unknown, but the engraving and the inscription suggest English origin. The date '1679' is inscribed on the flat base.

This pomander is a reminder of living conditions during the reign of Charles II (1660–85). Disease and plague were rampant, and so perfumes and herbs were used to counteract obnoxious smells and ward off pestilence. The *memento mori*, in the form of a skull, was a reminder that life is fleeting and death inevitable. Two similar examples are to be found in the museum: MG 90, in the form of a gold coffin containing an enamelled-gold skeleton, and MG 91, a little gold book that shows a man and woman embracing.

Reliquary Chasse

French, Limoges, early 13th century
Champlevé enamelled bronze plaques,
H 14.5 × W 13 × D 7
Accession no: HCM 080

This resplendent medieval chasse, designed to enshrine the sacred relics of a saint, is constructed of riveted alloy plaques on a metal base plate in a stylised church form with hinged roof. The cresting and zoomorphic feet are fifteenth century, the crocketed gables nineteenth-century additions. The iconography is consistent with the legend and cult of Martial, martyr and patron saint of Limoges, whose sanctuary was among the most venerated in twelfth-century Christendom. The narrative to the front depicts Christ in Majesty within a mandorla, flanked by angels. A soldier wearing contemporary dress decapitates the kneeling martyr. A standing saint represents the apotheosis of Martial's soul.

These engraved figures have cast-appliqué heads. The obverse decoration, a diaper of four petalled flowers inscribed within circles, is repeated in double rows. Each gable end frames an unidentified saint within grids.

The devotional imagery is set against brilliant-blue enamelled ground using the champlevé technique. Fired vitrified powder and oxides fused permanent colour to metal cells and roundels, which, when burnished, enhanced the magnificence of the reliquary. Limoges, well positioned for commerce and pilgrimage routes, became the most productive centre of ecclesiastical enamels with the largest surviving corpus of metalwork from the Middle Ages. The decorative scheme, drawing from early medieval art and manuscript illumination, with dynamic animation and displaying Romanesque stylisation, dates this chasse to the early thirteenth century.

Reliquary Cross, known as the Mary, Queen of Scots, Crucifix

Spanish or English, *c.*1590
Gold, partly enamelled, H 5.5 × W 3 × D I
Accession no: MG 095

The cross has a three-dimensional enamelled Corpus Christi and skull, with an INRI inscription band on the front, engraved instruments of the passion and an enamelled heart and crown of thorns on the back. The sides bear the engraved inscription: 'Beholde who suffere what and for whom he suffered'. The cross is hinged at the top so that the hollow interior, which would have originally held a religious relic, may be revealed.

The cross is of a common type, but particularly associated with the Counter-Reformation in Spain. The inscription suggests that either the patron who commissioned it, or a subsequent owner, was English. It is anecdotally linked to Mary, Queen of Scots (1542–87), but in fact there is no direct link with her. Inventories of her jewellery, the latest dating to 1562, do not include any crosses, though it is known that at the sad end of her life she had some in her possession. The cross is contained in an early shagreen covered case.

Ringed Pins

Viking, 10th–11th century
Copper alloy, l from 12.2 to 17.2
Accession nos: HCA 523; 520; 522; MGO 063

These four ringed pins are dated to the Viking-age. They functioned as simple dress fasteners and essentially consist of pins with separate swivel rings inserted in their heads. Several different types of ringed pins are known, differentiated from one another on the basis of the form of their pinheads and rings. Two of the examples included here belong to the plain-ringed class (HCA 523 and 520), while the others are kidney-ringed in form; all four examples feature polyhedral-headed pins. Engraving or stamping decorates the objects, with particular attention paid to the pinheads. Simple interlaced twin-link motifs occur in this position on two of the pins (HCA 520 and MGO 63).

It has been suggested that plain- and kidney-ringed pins were manufactured in Viking Dublin, from where many examples have been excavated. There the evidence indicates that the plain-ringed type was being produced largely in the mid-tenth century, while the kidney-ringed form developed during the late tenth century and continued in use throughout the eleventh. Examples of both these types of ringed pins are occasionally found on native Irish sites, while the plain-ringed type is also discovered in Viking contexts on the Faeroes and Iceland. Such pins, therefore, provide evidence for a Hiberno-Norse involvement in the Viking settlement of the North Atlantic region.

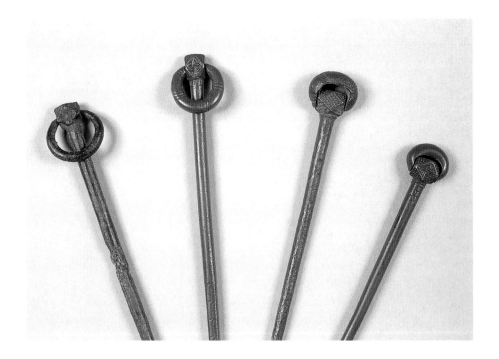

The Antrim Cross

Irish, first half 9th century
Cast bronze, enamel, H 16.8 × w 16.4
Accession no: HCA 627

The Antrim Cross is the most important Irish antiquity in the Hunt Collection, named after the county where it was found many years ago. Its equal arms would once have been decorated with metal plaques and now form graceful concave curves that terminate in raised bosses in the form of a truncated pyramid. The latter's sloping sides are decorated with interlocking angular fields of yellow enamel, alternating with a similar-coloured design of an arrow within a truncated triangle. The pyramidal boss at the centre is taller and has angular enamelled panels on two of its four sides. The other two sides, back to back, differ in that they are attractively decorated with an animal design, once fully enamelled between its raised outlines. The legs of the animal are tucked up beneath its body, and its head – with widely open mouth – turns back towards its tail. The flat tops of the bosses are decorated with small squares of *millefiori* enamel. Rivet-holes in the separately cast base-plate show that this cross was attached to a flat (possibly wooden) surface, quite probably of a house-shaped reliquary like the twelfth-century example from Lemanaghan, County Offaly.

The importance of the Antrim Cross lies in the fact that it is the only virtually intact example of its kind and period – though there were others, as we know from comparable enamelled bosses looted by the Vikings and placed in their Norwegian graves, including one in the Oseberg ship burial that occurred shortly after AD 834. This gives a likely date of *c.* AD 800–50 for the Antrim Cross.

Berlin Ironwork Tiara and Necklace

Prussian, Berlin,
c.1825 (tiara),
1825–50 (necklace)

Cast and enamelled iron,
Diam. 16.5 (tiara) – L 44.5
(necklace)

Accession nos: HCL 011;
HM 1998.1

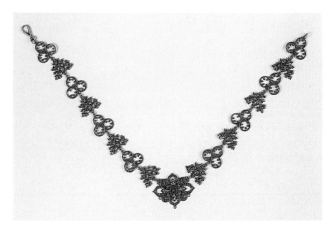

Berlin ironwork jewellery was first produced in Silesia at the end of the eighteenth century. It was first made in Berlin, with other larger-scale iron goods, after the Royal Berlin Foundry opened there in 1804. Napoleon captured the city in 1806 and removed the factory's casts to Paris. During the campaign of liberation against Napoleon (1813–15), the wealthy were encouraged to donate their precious jewellery to the war effort and were given Berlin iron jewellery in exchange, often inscribed with a patriotic motto such as *Gold gab ich für Eisen* (I gave gold for iron). At this time Berlin iron jewellery production was at its height and it continued until the mid-nineteenth century, exhibited in the Great Exhibitions of 1851 and 1861. The neoclassical motifs, which had been popular in the early years of manufacture, gave way to neo-Gothic design, especially after the defeat of Napoleon.

Karl Friedrich Schinkel was the foremost designer in the latter style. The skill of the work was basically in the casting. Motifs such as the trilobe and trifoliate shapes, which can be seen on both pieces, recur frequently. The work is often stamped with the name of the foundry, such as Geiss, Lehmann, Hossauer & Devarenne of Berlin and Schott of Ilsenburg am-Harts. The unmarked necklace closely resembles stamped work by Geiss.

Pap Boat Feeding Vessel

Irish, Limerick, Joseph Johns, *c.*1760
Sterling silver, L 10
Accession no: HCL 006

This is a small, shallow vessel, similar in
shape to a sauceboat, with a long, wide lip
convenient for those who are too weak to
feed themselves. Pap is said to be the
sound a baby makes when hungry or while
it is feeding, and the word applies to soft or
semi-liquid food given to infants and
invalids. Not many Pap boats were made
in Ireland: two were registered at the
Dublin assay office in 1788 and then none
until 1810.

This pap boat is made of silver and
devoid of decoration. The mark of Joseph
Johns, a lion rampant, is struck twice on
the bottom accompanied by the paired
initials 'W' and 'I', which may indicate a
wedding or christening gift. Johns'
initials 'II', on either side of the lion, are
accompanied by the word Sterling. Johns
had a workshop on Mary Street in
Limerick's English town. He was elected
Mayor of Limerick in 1773 and died two
years later.

Knobbed Bronze Armlet and Cast-bronze Torque

Iron Age, La Tène period
Bronze, Diam. 7.5 (HCA 441); 14.5 (HCA 454)
Accession nos: HCA 441 (armlet); 454
(torque)

These are just two of a large number of objects from the Celtic Iron Age that can be seen in the Museum. The knobbed bronze armlet is cast with rounded terminals, and alternating thick and narrow projections. It is hollow and C-shaped in cross-section. The decoration is distinctive and occurs on Central European armlets, bracelets and neck-rings, most commonly in Hungary and former Czechoslovakia, where such objects have been found in Celtic grave groups. Thinner examples occur in the Marne area of France. This armlet is very similar to an Iron Age bracelet also in the Museum.

The cast-bronze two-piece Celtic torque is a very finely made example of a type found almost exclusively in north-eastern Britain and southern Scotland. It has a flat ring that becomes circular towards the centre, and a separate lower section decorated with melon-shaped 'beads'. This pseudo-beaded torque is cast in two pieces. It is based on torques with separate beads and spacers on separate curved pieces of metal. The ring and the beads both bear cast decoration consisting of stipples, meandering lines, diagonal strokes and parallel lines. Only one such torque, with separate beads, has been found in Ireland – an import to Lambay Island off the Dublin coast.

Salver or Card Tray

Irish, Limerick, Joseph Johns, *c.*1750
Sterling silver, Diam. 22
Accession no: HCL 001

This circular tray with a pie-crust edge and shell border stands on three pad feet. Inside the border is a flat-chased decoration of fruit and flowers. The tray bears on the back the mark of Joseph Johns, a lion rampant, with the initials 'II' on either side accompanied by the word 'sterling', showing that it is of sterling standard, made up of at least 925 parts fine per 1,000 with the remainder being copper. Silver being a soft metal, it needs to be hardened by copper to facilitate its manufacture and ensure that the object retains its shape during many years of use. As Limerick never had an assay office it must be taken on trust that the tray is of sterling standard.

Salver is from the Spanish word *salva*, meaning the tray from which the king's taster sampled food before serving it, but smaller ones, such as this, are known as card trays, used for the reception of calling cards. In the centre is the crest of the Russell family, descended from Philip, born in 1650, whose members included a mayor and a member of parliament. Their burial place was at St John's, Limerick, where there are four vaults and a mausoleum all bearing the family crest.

Granta Fen Torque

English, Late Bronze Age, c.1200–1000 BC
Gold, L 110.5, weight 120 g
Accession no: HCA 419

This torque was found with a cache of other objects of gold and bronze in 1850 in a bog at Granta Fen, Cambridgeshire, England. It found its way into the possession of Lord Londesborough, but at the auction of his collection in 1884 the hoard was dispersed. The torque was bought by General Sir Pitt-Rivers and displayed at his museum at Farnham in Dorset. From there it came into the Hunt Collection. The remainder of the find, which consisted of a gold bracelet, six gold-ribbed rings and a fragment of a bronze rapier, was acquired by the British Museum, London.

The practice of twisting bars of gold was established in western Europe by about 1200 BC, probably as a result of influences from the east Mediterranean and the Baltic. By hammering up the angles on bars of square, rectangular or triangular shape, flanges are produced of cruciform, X- or Y-shaped section. The bar is then twisted to produce a flange-twisted torque. This is an extremely fine example, made from a bar with four flanges that has been very evenly twisted. This level of control of the metal requires considerable skill and highly developed goldsmithing skills. Some torques of this type have been coiled, possibly in an effort to reduce their size for ease of concealment or, perhaps, as part of the ritual of final deposition in the ground. Similar torques are known from Ireland, the most important being the pair found at Tara, County Meath.

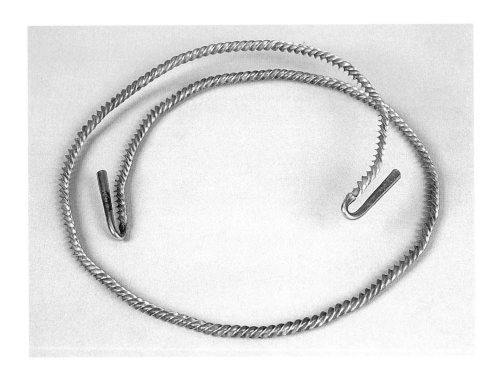

'Pendants' or Y-shaped Pieces

Irish, Iron Age, 2nd or 1st century BC
Cast bronze, H (HCA 463) 30.8; H (HCA 464) 30.3
Accession nos: HCA 463; 464

Almost identical, these objects belong to a class of artefact once referred to as a 'Y-shaped piece' but now normally described as a 'pendant'. On each, the stem has at its end a simple pear-shaped knob, while each prong ends in a hollowed terminal with a loop cast at a right angle to it. The occasional association of pendants with horse-bits suggests that in some way they functioned as harness attachments. A number have been found in pairs (as in this case), implying that they came from the harness-set of a pair of horses, such as would be necessary for a chariot or cart.

Possibly they served to lead or hold horses whose reins were inaccessible from the front.

The Y-shaped pendant is peculiar to Ireland, which is surprising in that other artefacts belonging to the Irish Iron Age, including the horse-bits, have close ancestors in Britain and Celtic Europe. This particular type of pendant, classified as type 1a, is associated with horse-bits that can be dated to the second or first century BC. The County Limerick provenance of this pair is outside the area – the northern half of Ireland – in which most have been found. Local manufacture, however, is indicated by the fact that the casting seam on one of the pendants has not been completely cleaned away.

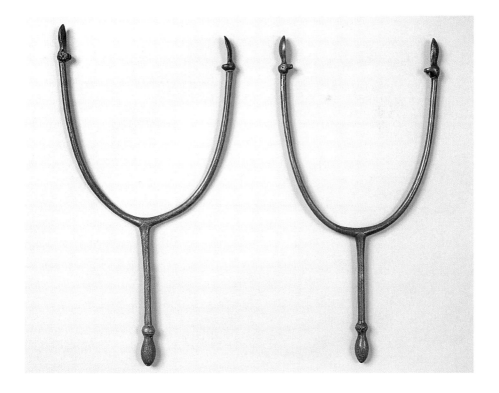

Ballyscullion Cauldron

Irish, Late Bronze Age
Bronze, H 57 × Diam. 57
Accession no: HCA 458

The body and rim of this cauldron are made from eight pieces of beaten bronze, each hammered to a thickness of about 1 mm and riveted together. The horizontal rows of conical-headed rivets on the exterior are both functional and decorative. The handles are each made of four pieces of bronze: a cast circular ring of complex ribbed cross-section, a sheet-bronze ribbed and flanged U-shaped tube and two other sheet-bronze half-tubes riveted to the rim edges. The rim was strengthened by the attachment of eight vertical slender bronze stays riveted to the body exterior. All but one of these are broken, suggesting that the rim was at one time subjected to quite a load in the past. The interior of the base displays many small, irregular indentations, as if hit repeatedly by a hard object.

In Late Bronze Age Europe, about 800 BC, similar cauldrons were the prestigious possessions of the élite, probably used in great feasting or drinking ceremonies. Careful and frequent repairs show they were highly prized, and, in Ireland, when their functional life was over, most were deposited in watery places, such as bogs, as votive offerings to the gods. Unearthed in 1880, in Ballyscullion, County Antrim, this cauldron was acquired by T. W. U. Robinson and later purchased by the Pitt-Rivers Museum, then in Dorset, now Oxford.

Rearing Horse

Italian, after Leonardo da Vinci, 16th century
Bronze, H 20.5 × W 12 × D 23
Accession no: MG 037

This horse has been linked to a sheet of Leonardo da Vinci's drawings of horses in the Royal Library, Windsor Castle, England. The drawings represent Leonardo's first thoughts for the *Battle of Anghiari* wall painting, a major commission from the Florentine Republic in 1503. They reveal his creative approach to a traditional theme, his expression of the conflict through such dynamic figures as the rearing horses.

The Hunt Museum bronze retains much of the expressive power of Leonardo's drawing. On another sheet of drawings for this painting, beside a sketch of a horse with a stance similar to that of this horse, is Leonardo's note to 'make from it a small [model] in wax about one

dito [10 cm] long'. He had done so earlier for the Sforza bronze equestrian monument. Whether this horse was cast from a scaled-up clay model in Florence, or modelled in the Milan workshop of the scupltor Pompeo Leoni (who owned Leonardo's drawings towards the end of the sixteenth century) is debatable. This is one of four similar small, bronze, rearing horses, after Leonardo; the other three being in the Metropolitan Museum of Art, New York, the Museum of Fine Arts, Budapest and the Jeannerat collection, London.

Bronze Age Shield

Irish, Late Bronze Age
Bronze, Diam. 65
Accession no: HCA 457

This circular shield is made of very thin sheet-bronze, evenly beaten to a thickness of less than 1 mm. It is skilfully and symmetrically decorated with 11 concentric repoussé ribs and 11 rows of low hemispherical bosses. A large, hollow central boss is stepped and of a rounded conical shape. Two neat circular perforations, replacing bosses in one row, held the rivets for suspension tabs, now missing. A central handle, on the back, is a stout, C-sectioned strip of bronze, held in place by two rivets with heads indistinguishable from the decorative bosses. Six tears or holes represent damage from the rear; one irregular perforation represents damage from the front, and it is unclear what

might have caused this. Some indentations on the exterior of the central boss were also produced from the front.

It is unlikely, however, that this object was ever used in combat. Experimentation with modern replicas shows that it would have been easily penetrated with bronze weaponry. This shield, like many others known in later Bronze Age Europe, was made for display and, along with sword and spear, was part of the trappings of aristocratic warriors. It was they who probably participated in the feasting and drinking ceremonies associated with cauldrons and buckets. Its find spot is unknown, but it may have come from County Antrim and was in the collection of T. W. U. Robinson in the nineteenth century and then sold to the Pitt-Rivers Museum, Oxford.

Decorative Hand Warmer

English, 12th century
Bronze, H 10
Accession no: HCM 159

The hand warmer is a practical piece of design, appealing to both the eye and the sense of touch. This was the most common form in use in the late Middle Ages. Its two halves unscrew to reveal a small, plain, iron cup that served as a container for the red-hot charcoal, balanced so that it remained upright whatever its position. The clever design of the hand warmer provided heat without scorching, and, unlike the modern-day pocketsize version, this example was large enough to warm both hands at once.

Hand warmers were used especially, though not exclusively, by priests during the celebration of Mass. In the eleventh century increased care was devoted to the handling of the Sacrament, lest numb fingers should accidentally drop the host or spill the chalice, a mishap that merited a stern punishment. A hand warmer might be found in every well-appointed church. Made from cast bronze, this is a fine example of a functional yet decorative metal object, in which the foliate decoration, of curling leaves and tendrils, and the sphere-shaped form are perfectly integrated.

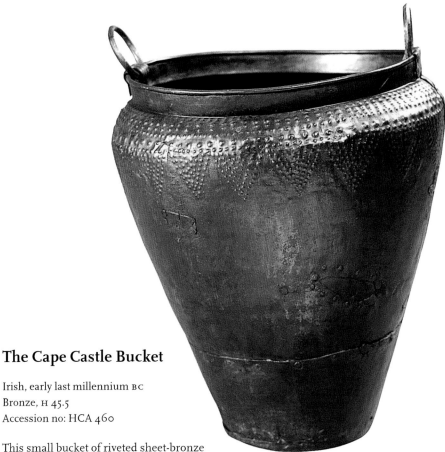

The Cape Castle Bucket

Irish, early last millennium BC
Bronze, H 45.5
Accession no: HCA 460

This small bucket of riveted sheet-bronze has a tub-shaped lower piece, its concave base protected by a wheel-shaped base-plate. The upper portion is made of two sheets of bronze riveted together with flat-headed rivets. The neck is vertical with a rolled rim. The bucket has been much repaired on both base and body: one riveted internal patch covers a large hole in the body; there are external patches and several very rough repairs to the base. The handles are lozenge-sectioned circular rings, which ride freely in ribbed staples (which may be replacements) riveted to the neck. A distinctive feature is the repoussé decoration on the upper body, a horizontal band of rows of low bosses on the shoulder with filled pendant triangles

below. This sort of decoration is known on continental buckets of the last millennium BC but is rarely found on Irish-British metalwork.

The maker of this vessel was evidently familiar with foreign bucket fashions. Like the Ballyscullion Cauldron, this was a highly prized and much repaired status symbol, probably used in drinking ceremonies. Found in Cape Castle bog, near Armoy, County Antrim, it was formerly in the possession of William Gray, in the collection of T. W. U. Robinson from 1881 and purchased in 1890 by the Pitt-Rivers Museum.

Galway Chalice

Irish, c.1630
Silver, H 21.8
Accession no: HCM 116

The most distinct feature of this seventeenth-century travelling chalice is its
domed octagonal foot design, which
distinguishes it from the incurved-
pyramoidal style more commonly found
on Roman Catholic chalices of this period.
This unusual design allows the cup and
stem, when unscrewed, to fit snugly into
the foot thus allowing ease of transport.
The cast balustral stem has screw threads
of different sizes at either end to ensure
that the knop cannot be inverted when the
chalice is reassembled. One facet of the
foot has an engraved crucifixion scene
with the INRI *titulus* above and a raised
calvary below. The letters 'FTD' are
engraved at the foot of the cross.

Two chalices of similar design are
recorded in J. J. Buckley's *Some Irish Altar
Plate* (1943), and one of these, the
Elizabeth Forth Chalice, has a knop
identical to this example and an inscribed
date of 1633 with a Galway provenance.
John Hunt believed that both knops came
from the same mould and thus dated this
chalice to c.1630. The slightly incurved
vertical member at the base of the foot
has a continuous chevron with pellets,
both in relief, which is similar to the
decoration on many chalices of the early
seventeenth century. The plain deep
bowl has the maker's mark 'EG' punched
below the straight rim. This mark also
occurs on the 'Galway Sword'
and a Galway pyx, and
may well be the mark
of an unknown Galway
maker.

Penal Cross

Irish, *c.*1829
Lead, H 9.7 × W 3.9 × D 2.4
Accession no: HCM 071

Penal crosses were made in Ireland
throughout the eighteenth century and
early nineteenth. Mostly made of wood,
they represent the main corpus of Irish
folk art from this period. Although the
crosses served as a focus of religious
devotion among an impoverished
population, their original source of
production was Lough Derg, County
Mayo, where they were sold in large
quantity to pilgrims who visited there.
This rare example is one of only four lead
penal crosses recorded. It possesses some
of the defining features of the wooden
crosses, such as the short arms, the figure
of Christ in high relief on the obverse and
the sacred inscription 'IHS' on the
reverse. However, it lacks the usual abun-
dance of Passion symbols. There are some
schematic parallel lines on both sides of
the lower shaft, which are similar to the
degraded representations of the ladder on
some of the later wooden crosses.

Generally the earlier crosses were
carved in a more naturalistic fashion than
this one, and with finer detail. Although
this example has a well-defined fan-shaped
halo and the elongated figure of Christ is
in high relief, the hands, face and crossed
feet are ill defined and more representative
of the degeneration of the later examples.
This suggests that the faint incised date
on the reverse face, which seems to read
'1829', is probably the correct date of
the cross.

Wine Strainer

Roman, 1st century AD
Bronze, L 27.3 × Diam. (ext.) 14 × H 9.3
Accession no: HCA 678

This short-handled, sheet-bronze wine strainer was used as a cooking utensil. It has a round-bottomed bowl with steep, straight sides and an outward-curving rim. A flat handle with hidden joints curves and narrows then widens towards the outer end. The handle is punctured with a crescent-shaped opening for hanging. The hanging detail is derived from two swanlike birds placed back to back, as seen in other examples of strainer handles from Herculaneum. The main body is perforated with a series of small holes forming a decorative pattern. The straining holes on the sides comprise two double sets of concentric rings framing an interlocking rectangular-meander pattern. A rosette motif of four petals and four dots at the centre of each petal decorates the base. Other first-century AD examples from Pompeii and Herculaneum, taken together with a recent strainer find from the Roman province of Noricum, provide stylistic comparisons for the first-century AD.

Dodecahedron

1st–4th century AD
Bronze, H 4.9
Accession no: HCM 157

This 12-sided bronze object has 12 circular
holes of different diameters set within 12
equal pentagons, which are marked by
spherical projections of equal size at each
corner. Concentric grooves are forged
around the holes of each of the 12 faces.
At least 45 such objects have been found in
the northern provinces of the Roman
Empire, yet there is no mention of them
in classical sources and their purpose
remains unclear.

Several suggestions as to the function of
this dodecahedron have been made. Some
believe it to be a gaming piece or dice,
others claim it as a candleholder (wax has
been found in one example from
Germania) or a sceptre head. Others see it
as a version of a game, in which each knob
represents a place in the world, whereby a
thread passed through each hole was a way
of travelling the globe. Most scholars,
however, favour the suggestion that it was
used as a measuring device, as an ancient
surveying instrument, a theory supported
by the hole in each diametrically opposite
face that is proportionally related to the
other, although never the same size. It is
therefore possible to determine ratios
from looking through the holes and
aligning sight with a distant object.

Zoomorphic Penannular Brooch

Irish, Ballymoney, Co. Antrim, 6th century
Enamelled copper alloy, Diam. (of ring) 4.9
Accession no: HCA 509

This brooch has a plain, round-sectioned hoop and flattened, expanded terminals. Each terminal has a sub-triangular cell containing an equal-armed cross with expanded ends set in reserved metal. In each case the cross arm flanking the opening ends in a small loop to form a chi-rho monogram: 'XP', the first two letters of *Christos*, Christ's name in Greek. The enamel on the terminals is modern. The junction between the hoop and terminal is decorated with a chevron pattern. The pinhead is plain.

The zoomorphic penannular brooch (so-called because of the stylised animal heads at the junction of hoop and terminal) was developed in the third and fourth centuries by British metalworkers, who combined Roman forms with motifs and techniques of the later Iron Age and Roman period. Archaeological finds indicate that the type was introduced to the east of Ireland – the area most prone to external influences and contacts – from south-west Britain. Its adoption in Ireland suggests that Roman forms of dress were also introduced. While the type appears to have gone out of use in Britain by the fifth century, it continued to be developed in Ireland into the sixth. Explicit Christian iconography is rare on such objects. The cross form is found on the *Cathach*, the earliest dated Irish manuscript, *c.* AD 600. This particular brooch is unique in that the crosses take the form of chi-rho motifs. The earliest use for this type of motif is the sixth century, the closest parallels occurring on the early seventh-century *Codex Usserianus Primus* and on cross-inscribed pillars of a similar date.

Handpin

6th century
Enamelled copper alloy, L 16.75
Accession no: HCA 533

This type of dress pin is known as a handpin, its head resembling the palm of the
hand with the fingers bent forward. Like
the zoomorphic penannular brooches, this
form of small dress pin originated in late
Roman Britain and was later developed by
Irish craftsmen. The earliest handpins are
of silver and are of relatively modest size.
Examples in copper alloy, with elaborately
decorated heads and exceptionally long
pins, are regarded as being typologically
late in the series and were made in Ireland
into the sixth century. Most developed
handpins have five 'fingers' rather than
three as here. In this example the head
is a semicircular plate with a circular
perforation. It is capped by three
projecting fingers and is fixed to a right-
angled projection at the top of the shank.
The head is decorated with a pattern of
reserved metal against a background of red
enamel. The design consists of a pair of
inward-curving 'dodo' heads springing
from a central inverted U-shape.

Related stick pins with equally long and
thick shanks but disc-shaped heads are
also known. Such exceptionally long pins
(some are up to 30 cm in length) are
unknown in the previous Iron Age and
did not reappear until the tenth century.
They clearly functioned in a different
way to the contemporary zoomorphic
penannular brooches and must have been
used to fasten coarsely woven garments,
perhaps of wool.

Processional Cross

English, c.1450
Gilt copper alloy, H 62
(without base)
Accession no: HCM 062

This processional cross of cast and gilt copper alloy is mounted on a modern wooden base. The outline of the cross is decorated with projecting sprays of leaves and terminates in circular medallions, bearing separately applied symbols of three of the Evangelists; that of Mathew at the base is missing. The cross is soldered to a wrythen knop with lozenge-shaped projections, which is in turn set on a tapering socket. The bearded figure of Christ is riveted to the cross. He is shown clad in a loincloth, the crown of thorns represented by a ribbed fillet. The cross bears geometric engraved ornament on the front and back, the backs of the medallions engraved with a Tudor rose. Two empty sockets at the base of the cross may have originally held figures of the mourning Virgin and St John.

The presence of a socket indicates that this was a processional cross, designed so that it could be removed from the altar and mounted on a long staff, thereby enabling it to be carried about. There are a number of such crosses in the Victoria and Albert Museum, London, one of which may even be by the same artist. English processional and altar crosses of this type were made in large numbers and exported. There are numerous examples from Ireland, one of which is preserved in Braga Cathedral in north Portugal. Similar crosses were in use in later medieval Ireland – the finest Irish example being the Ballylongford Cross made in 1479. The example here, however, is English.

Pegasus Brooch

Western European, late 16th century
Enamelled gold set with cabochon ruby and
cut diamonds, H 3.5 × W 5
Accession no: T 021

Late sixteenth-century jewellery was
essentially sculptural, influenced by the
rediscovery of classical work. It was most
typically of enamelled gold with stones
used as an accent in the design rather
than its focus. Stonecutting was in its
infancy, and the inability to cut diamonds
effectively meant that other stones, such as
the ruby seen here on the body of Pegasus,
were more greatly prized. The Pegasus
brooch would originally have been the
focal part of a pendant jewel, which, by the
late sixteenth century, had taken over from
the cap badge as the dominant form of
jewellery. It would have hung, probably
with other decorative elements, by chains

from a ring attachment, which would have
been worn on a ribbon or chain around the
neck, or attached to the bodice or sleeve as
a brooch. Animal and bird motifs were
popular and widespread, typically of
enamelled gold, often white, as here, and
frequently incorporating an irregularly
shaped baroque pearl.

It is not possible to pinpoint the source
of the jewel since comparable work was
produced throughout western Europe, and
workmen and pattern books moved from
country to country. The animals were
often exotic, imaginary or from Classical
mythology, as in the case of Pegasus, the
winged horse, the offspring of Poseidon
and Medusa, tamed by the hero
Bellerophon.

Five-decade Rosary

Irish, 18th century
Silver, amber, L 49
Accession no: HCM 146

The use of beads for counting prayers is
widely practised in many religions.
Various forms were used by early
Christians, and by the twelfth century the
use of beads for counting the paternoster –
the Our Father or Lord's Prayer – was
widespread. The promotion of the rosary
from the Latin *rosarium*, rose garden, to a
series of prayers counted on a string of
beads is credited to the Dominican friars
of the fifteenth century. Various forms of
the rosary were used, but its essence
was the decade or ten Ave (Hail Mary)
separated by a *Pater* (*Pater Noster*, Our
Father). The date of its introduction to
Ireland is unclear, but by the seventeenth

century it was well established as both a
private and a household prayer.

Many Irish rosaries are referred to as
'Galway Rosaries' and typically bear a
strong Spanish stylistic influence. This
five-decade example has amber Aves, of
various shapes, and silver spherical *Paters*
strung together. The 7.5 cm long silver
cross is made from two intersecting silver
tubes with turned ends. There is a green
tassel at the end of the cross, but those
from the ends of the transom are no longer
extant. This type of tasselled tubular cross
is typical of the Galway Rosary. The figure
of the crucified Christ, which is attached
to the cross, is quite worn and has the
INRI *titulus* overhead. The letter 'H' and
figure '2' are inscribed on the reverse face
of the cross.

Wood, textiles and leather

Apollo

German, 17th century
Polychromed limewood, H 119
Accession no: HCM 013

Apollo, the Classical god of light, poetry,
music, healing and prophecy, was
often used to represent the trades,
arts and professions. Here he is
their protector; many of the crafts
and manual skills are represented
on the lower body, with music given
pride of place in the centre, and the
various other professions shown above.
In his right hand Apollo carries the
serpent and pestle, symbols of the art of
healing. In the left is a pomegranate, its
many seeds encased in a single skin,
symbolising, perhaps, the multitude of
activities presided over by a single deity,
each dependent on the daily and seasonal
solar cycle.

Augsburg, where the figure originated,
was famous for its music and musical
instruments; not surprisingly, these are
well represented. Drum and drumstick,
violin, viola, harp, tambourine, bagpipes,
panpipes, mandolin, whistle and
harpsichord are all shown. Equally
evident are the arts and skills of the
gamekeeper, including arrows, spears,
horn, baskets and beaters, as well as
their targets of fish and duck.

Beaufort, Turenne and Comminges Tapestry Fragment

French, 14th century, c.1370
Wool, H 93 × W 127.5
Accession no: HCL 017

This is a highly restored tapestry bearing the coats of arms of the Beaufort, Turenne and Comminges families. This fragment is part of a larger series, of which other portions survive in the Burrell Collection, Glasgow; the Metropolitan Museum of Art, New York; the Rijksmuseum, Amsterdam and elsewhere. Tapestries in this period were extremely expensive and a symbol of the wealth and status of their owners. This tapestry was most likely made for Guillaume Rogier III, Comte de Beaufort, his wife, Aliènor de Comminges, and their son Raymond, Vicomte de

Turenne. Rogier became rector of the papal city of Avignon when his brother was made Pope Gregory XI in 1370.

The design uses a repeating pattern, where, alternately, a lion, stag, elephant or unicorn, bearing a heraldic shield, is placed in the centre. Each animal is enclosed on the top by angels bearing a crown and on the bottom by turreted walls, possibly those of Avignon. This is enclosed in turn by rosettes and stylised storks, the latter a symbol of St Agricola, first bishop of Avignon. The walls and storks may represent the physical and spiritual protection afforded to the city, while the coats of arms indicate the armed force available to protect it and the papacy in times of danger.

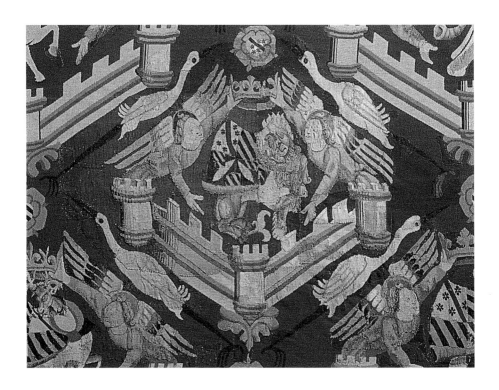

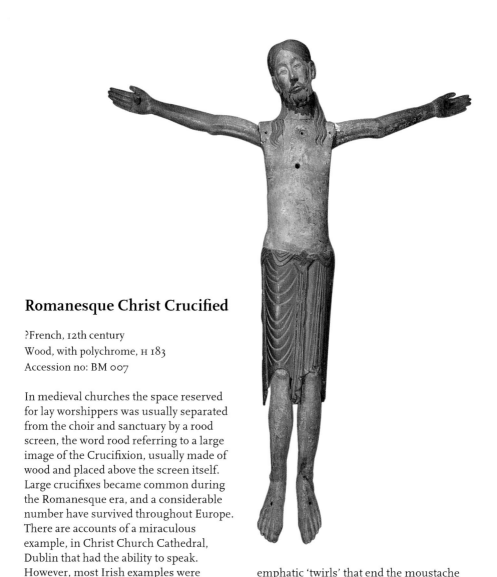

Romanesque Christ Crucified

?French, 12th century
Wood, with polychrome, H 183
Accession no: BM 007

In medieval churches the space reserved for lay worshippers was usually separated from the choir and sanctuary by a rood screen, the word rood referring to a large image of the Crucifixion, usually made of wood and placed above the screen itself. Large crucifixes became common during the Romanesque era, and a considerable number have survived throughout Europe. There are accounts of a miraculous example, in Christ Church Cathedral, Dublin that had the ability to speak. However, most Irish examples were destroyed at the Reformation.

This crucifix is deliberately elongated, with an emphasis on geometrical pattern, a feature characteristic of Romanesque art. The sculptor employed a number of obvious stylistic 'tricks': these include the overlapping flaps of the loincloth around the waist, the curious diamond-shaped knot in the centre, the way the loincloth has slipped below the level of the waist and the irregular hemline. Note also the emphatic 'twirls' that end the moustache and beard. The overall impact is highly expressive, and the slight bend in the head conveys a sense of sympathy, under-standing and thought. Despite the stylisation of the carving there are hints of naturalism, as in the subtle definition of the hips, which evoke the humanity of Christ. While the wound in the side (and the nail holes) suggest suffering, the open eyes remind the spectator that this is ultimately an image of triumph and hope.

Romanesque Enthroned Madonna

German, Lower Rhine, early 12th century
Polychromed limewood, H 65.3 × W 33 × D 19
Accession no: HCM 001

This Romanesque statue, of the Enthroned
Madonna, shows Mary as Theotokos
(Mother of God), or *Sedes Sapientiae* (the
Seat of Wisdom). Such works usually show
the Christ child on Mary's knee. His
absence from this example is tantalisingly
marked by the fixing dowels in Mary's lap.
He would probably have been shown as a
child-size man, while his mother is
depicted as a woman full of years and
wisdom. The impression is one of remote
majesty and monumental calm,
and is clearly not intended as a
normal mother-and-child scene.

Mary's pose is frontal, solemn
and hieratic. She is seated on a
high-backed throne, decorated
with flowers and geometric
motifs on three sides, with the
back undecorated and hollowed
out to prevent the wood from
cracking. Mary is dressed in a
fine red gown, gathered into an
elaborate belt, with a brooch at
her neck and a richly
embroidered blue mantle.
Her long, oval face, together
with some foreshortening of the
neck and upper body, suggest
that this statue was intended to
be viewed from below; many of
these madonnas were made to
stand on altars or plinths.
They were also designed for
mobility, often carried in
processions and used in
liturgical dramas, such as the
Epiphany plays.

Carving of the Flight into Egypt

?French, pre-1500
Polychromed wood,
H 70.05 × W 70
Accession no:
HCM 004

Mary rides the donkey, side-saddle, holding the child Jesus, who is partly draped in white. She wears a dark blue mantle and veil over a beige gown, gathered at the neck, and pointed shoes. She supports the child with her hands; he has one arm around her neck, while the other holds on to her veil. The large donkey, which is shod, has a crupper under its tail, which suggests a saddle, though there is no girth. There is a leather head-collar, and the reins are looped over Mary's thumb. Joseph, who walks in front, wears a brown belted garment, with a caped hood covering his shoulders, red hose and ankle boots with laced front openings. A buckled bag hangs from his belt. Joseph's forearms are missing, but a rope tied around the donkey's head at nose-band level and projecting between them suggests that he originally led the donkey.

This scene is recorded in St Matthew's gospel, with details from the apocryphal gospels, and was seen as the fulfilment of the Old Testament prophecy of Hosea. Such scenes more usually move from left to right, echoing the classical *adventus*, the coming of the emperor or other dignitary. The Flight was often paired with the Entry into Jerusalem. In one, the child travels to a heathen land where he is paid homage; in the other, he is welcomed as Messiah. This work is remarkably similar to an altarpiece panel painted in the 1470s by Michael Packer at St Wolfgang, near Salzburg, Austria.

Falconry Paraphernalia

Hawk's Hood
European, 19th or 20th century
Leather, velvet, feathers, wool, H 7.5
Accession no: HCM 137

Bell for Icelandic Gerfalcon
European, 17th century
Silver, H 4.3
Accession no: HCM 138

Hawk's Ring
European, 17th century
Silver, Diam. 1.9
Accession no: HCM 139

Hawk's Ring
European, 17th century
Silver, Diam. 1.2
Accession no: HCM 140

Hawk's Call or Whistle
European, 17th or 18th century
Wood, bone, leather, L 17
Accession no: HCM 141

All these items were used in falconry, a form of hunting with trained birds of prey. Originating c.1000 BC in the Asian steppes, falconry reached its peak in Europe during the Crusades of the eleventh, twelfth and thirteenth centuries, when it became a privilege and a symbol of nobility. Developments in weaponry in the seventeenth century greatly reduced the practical need for falconry, though it still retained enthusiastic followers.

A hood was used to keep a hunting bird quiet until release. This example may have been a product of the Mollen family of Valkenswaard, Holland, who made falconry equipment and supplied trained birds between 1820 and1930.

The bell, attached to a leg with a leather strip – a bewit – helped locate a lost bird. This large bell is engraved with the arms of King James I of England (1566–1625) and Ferdinand II, Holy Roman Emperor from 1619 to 1637.

The rings, known as varvels, as well as identifying the owner, prevented the bird from becoming entangled in the leash that attached it to its perch.

Birds were trained to return to the call or whistle, frequently made of wood, bone and leather, like this one.

Carving of a Man on Horseback

?Northern European, mid- to late 15th century
Oak, polychrome and gilding,
H 29 × W 25
Accession no: HCM 012

The man, in profile, is dark skinned with a full black beard and moustache; on his head he wears a red wide-brimmed, tasselled hat with a shallow crown and ear flaps; attached to the back of his hat, a knotted ribbon of gold material cascades down and across the back of the horse. Underneath his long golden cloak with wide collar may be seen traces of a loose blue undergarment, the tight sleeves of a tunic at his wrists, short red breeches, exposing his bare knee, above red leather boots with a loose cuff. His foot rests in a wide stirrup. In his right hand he holds the lower part of a lance – the upper section is missing – striped in red and white. His left arm, from which the hand is missing, is raised and curves toward his face. He appears to be looking up. The horse is black with a heavy mane and knotted tail, elaborately trapped in a gilded, tasselled caparison with double bit and bridle. It stands on a deeply ridged base, perhaps representing rough terrain.

It has been suggested that this carving may be a representation of St Longinus, one of a larger group depicting the Crucifixion, another example of which is to be found at the Cloisters in the Metropolitan Museum of Art, New York.

St Anne with the Christ Child and Virgin Mary

South German, c.1540
Polychromed limewood, H 107.5 × W 45
Accession no: MG 039

This elongated, mannerist St Anne, mother of the Virgin Mary, wears a heavily draped dark robe with traces of gilding and a red lining, a veil low on her forehead and a white wimple. She holds and looks down at the naked Christ child, whose hair is shown as flat spiral curls. Mary, who wears a green gown with a high belted waistline, reaches and looks up towards the child. Her missing right hand would originally have touched the child's foot in an affectionate gesture. She has a circular fillet on her head, but otherwise her very long brown hair is worn loose.

This image type has its origins in the cult of the Holy Kinship, the extended family of Christ, the descendants of St Anne from her three marriages. St Anne is not mentioned in the Bible, but legends of her come from the apocryphal gospels and the Golden Legend and echo the Old Testament story of Hannah, mother of Samuel. This type of image, while having no exact equivalent in English, is known in German as Anna Selbdritt and in French as Anne Trinitaire. It celebrated Christ's humanity as part of a kinship group, just as the more usual Trinity honoured his divinity. Martin Luther disapproved of legend-based religious images; the Council of Trent saw this image conflicting with the doctrine of Mary's Immaculate Conception, and so it was replaced by the Holy Family of Mary, Joseph and the Christ child.

St John the Evangelist

German or ?Spanish, 17th century
Pearwood, H 49 × W 18 × D 14
Accession no: MG 041

Also known as the Apostle, and the Beloved
Disciple, St John, son of Zebedee, is here
shown with an eagle, his attribute as one of
the four Evangelists. John wrote three short
epistles, the fourth gospel and finally the
Book of Revelation or Apocalypse. The eagle
has a scroll across its back painted with the
opening words of John's gospel, *In principio*,
meaning 'In the beginning'. The basis
of the eagle is the Old Testament vision of
Ezekiel. The figure is young and graceful,
with abundant long hair and beardless,
unlike most depictions of the other
Apostles. Whether as part of a Last Supper,
a Deposition or a Crucifixion, John is
unmistakable by his youth and somewhat
androgynous beauty. The only exception is
when he is shown as an old man writing his
Apocalypse in exile on Patmos.

Where all the Apostles have
distinguishing attributes, John is shown
holding a cup with a snake or dragon
emerging from it – referring to a legendary
failed attempt to poison him – so it is
possible that this figure once held a cup in
the now missing hands. This piece, with its
elegantly handled drapery and serene air,
owes a debt to the German Late Gothic
style of carving. Traditionally, St John
died at Ephesus between AD 96 and
104. As the founder of the Seven
Churches there, he is patron of Asia
Minor and, among many other groups,
of art dealers.

Two Dublin Tapestries

Irish, ?Richard Pawlet or Daniel
Reyley, c.1740–50
Peeckelhaering, H 52 × W 47.5
Wool, Scribe H 53 × W 48.7;
Accession nos: HCL 019; 020

These are two of the few known, surviving tapestry pieces of Dublin manufacture. Although one at least has been used as a chair seat, they were most likely produced as apprentice or competition samples. The pictorial subject matter, its treatment and the differing qualities of the two woven pieces make it unlikely that they would have been part of a set for use as furnishing. Both designs were based on prints that would have been available in Dublin at the time.

The drinker is inspired by Frans Hals' *Peeckelhaering* of the late 1620s, an image widely disseminated in books and prints.

The scribe copying a book is as yet unidentified. The weavers were probably Richard Pawlet or Daniel Reyley, apprentices to John van Beaver, a Fleming who executed the tapestries for the Irish House of Lords. Each tapestry bears similarities to his work, although the designs are less accomplished. The list of entries for the Dublin Society premiums from 1742 to 1754, given to John van Beaver, Daniel Reyley, Richard Pawlet and Philip Croye (Pawlet's journeyman), relates to the small scale and type of these two. Both tapestries remain in very good condition, with remarkably vivid colours that have not faded.

Statue of a Man

?Greek, 6th century BC
Wood, H 56
Accession no: MG 036

This is a most puzzling object of low
artistic but high scientific interest. The
half life-size figure has been damaged by
time and, further so, by the attachment of
a modern face. Traces of ancient piecing
also remain. The figure stands in a hieratic
fashion. In the details of its carving,
especially of the ear and the groove round
the head, and the fact that it was bearded,
the statue is closer to Greek work of the
later sixth century BC than Egyptian
figures, which are rarely depicted nude.
However, the preservation of a wooden
statue in most parts of the Greek world
would be rare; the few that have survived
are almost all from waterlogged ground,
unlike, it would appear, this *kouros*.

Investigation of a sample removed by
John Hunt (not wholly in accord with
modern museum guidelines) revealed
that the wood is of the *Acacia Negevensis*,
a south-east Mediterranean variety.
A carbon date obtained at the laboratory
of the British Museum gave a time of
c.2250 BC, the Egyptian twelfth dynasty.
The balance of judgement is fine, although
no Egyptologist has yet been ready to claim
the piece. A possible resolution of the
problem is that it was originally an artefact
of that early date, but that it was found
and reworked by a Greek carver many
centuries later. If so, it is the largest
known wood art object of the archaic and
Classical Greek periods.

Annunciation Canopy or Baldachin

?French or German, 15th century
Wood, H 135 × W 127
Accession no: HCM 083

This carved canopy bearing an Annunciation scene was possibly designed for a Lady Chapel. Above are traces of two angels, at least one of which swings a censer. It was most likely to have been positioned over a side altar reredos or used as a backdrop to a statue, and at one time may have abutted another piece of decorated woodwork. Traces of painted foliage survive.

The main panel seems to have been over-painted and thickly repainted in places.

The Archangel Gabriel appears to the Virgin Mary, shown with a book at a reading desk. The Holy Ghost, in the form of a dove, surrounded by rays of light, hangs between the main figures, as does a vase containing flowers, not a customary lily among them. The Archangel Gabriel and the Virgin Mary both have scrolls on which the words of the Archangel's salutation and the Virgin's response were recorded in black script. The lower register has two panels with open-work Gothic lettering proclaiming *'Ave Maria Gratia Plena'* (Hail Mary Full of Grace). Originally these were partially incised and painted. The woodwork is mortised and pegged.

Statue of Balthasar

South German, 16th century
Limewood, H 123
Accession no: HCM 010

This statue of Balthasar, one of the Magi,
is in good condition. Most of the original
polychrome (red, gold, green and black)
remains intact. Historically, the Magi were
astrologers of the Persian court. It was a
star that led them to the birthplace of
Christ in Bethlehem, where they offered
their gifts of gold, frankincense and myrrh.

The appearance of a star at the birth
of a ruler indicated divinity. While
Jewish shepherds were the first to
venerate the Christ Child, these wise
men represented the Gentiles. They do
not appear as kings in the earliest
drawings in the Roman catacombs.
Tertullian in the second century was the
first to call them kings, and from the tenth
century onwards they are thus represented
in the visual arts. The Magi were named
Balthasar, Caspar and Melchoir by Origen
in the third century, and the Venerable
Bede tells us that the three gifts symbolise
Tribute, Divinity and Suffering. In the
later Middle Ages, they came to personify
the three known continents: Europe,
Africa, and Asia. According to tradition,
their bones are preserved in an ornate
casket in the sanctuary of Cologne
Cathedral. Their feast, 6 January, still
brings pilgrims to honour the kings, just
as they honoured the Christ Child in
their day.

Methers or Drinking Vessels

Irish, 16th–17th century
Wood, H 17.5 to 8.7
Accession no: HCM 221-6

A mether is a two-piece wooden drinking vessel, usually carved from a single block of wood with a separate disc-like base inserted in a groove or croze. It is usually sub-rectangular at the mouth and tapers to a circular shape at the base. There are commonly between one and four undercut handles, but, in rare instances, none. The lug-like handles may extend either to the base or along just some of the height of the vessel, and sometimes they tend to help balance it. Ornament is invariably simple and geometric, and lightly incised. It is suggested that the form of the handles is derived from certain types of post-medieval pottery, but they may instead originate from the holed flanges left on the sides of the medieval, Irish bog butter churns and kegs, some of which have

similar decoration. In Ireland and Scotland the mether was also used for storing bog butter.

Some kegs are radiocarbon dated to between the thirteenth and the fifteenth century, while there are churns that have been dated to between the tenth and the twelfth century. However, the full date range for all such vessels is likely to be wider. Several have sixteenth- to eighteenth-century dates carved on them. There are accounts by English visitors, as early as the seventeenth century, of their use in Ireland. The mether was probably still being made up to the early nineteenth century, after which it became an object of antiquary interest. The term mether is itself antiquarian, and various spellings are used. This fine group is the Museum's entire holding of methers, representative of the range of forms and sizes of those found in Ireland.

Evening Gown

Irish, Sybil Connolly (1921–98), *c.*1968
Linen, L 123
Accession no: HM 1999.8

Maquette

Irish, Sybil Connolly (1921–98), *c.*1952
Linen, L 48
Accession no: HML 19.3

Sybil Connolly was a pioneering designer in Ireland and
among the first to enjoy international success. Her
lavender pleated-linen evening gown with frilled neckline, three-quarter length sleeves and straight skirt is
lined with pink satin stitched to the back of the pleated
linen. The maquette in cream pleated linen is a
miniature version of a strapless evening gown, known
as the 'First Love' dress. The bodice is trimmed at the
top with a satin ribbon in a criss-cross weave. The skirt
is in four tiers with borders of the ribbon between each.

Connolly was born in Wales, of an Irish father and
Welsh mother. She came to live in Ireland in her teens
and in 1938 went to London to study dress design at
Bradley's. On returning to Dublin she joined the firm of
Richard Alan, producing her first collection there in
1952. She became extremely successful, especially in the
USA, and set up on her own in Merrion Square, Dublin,
in 1957. She used traditional Irish textiles, such as
tweed, crochet and lace, turning them into high-fashion
garments. She was especially
celebrated for her use of linen,
which she pleated to produce a
delicate fabric; it took nine yards
of linen to produce one pleated
yard. Late in her career she
turned her attention to interior
decoration and designed crystal,
fabric and ceramics.

Stone

A Selection of Arrowheads

Leaf-shaped Arrowhead
Neolithic
Flint, L 4.6
Accession no: HCA 014

Leaf-shaped Arrowhead
Neolithic
Flint, L 4.4
Accession no: HCA 011

Leaf/Lozenge-shaped Arrowhead
Neolithic
Flint, L 3.9
Accession no: HCA 006

Lozenge-shaped Arrowhead
Neolithic
Flint, L 4.4
Accession no: HCA 017

Concave-based Arrowhead
Neolithic/Early Bronze Age
Flint, L 4.6
Accession no: HCA 025

Concave-based Arrowhead
Neolithic/Early Bronze Age
Flint, L 3.3
Accession no: HCA 029

Barbed-and-Tanged Arrowhead
Early Bronze Age
Flint, L 2.8
Accession no: HCA 038

Barbed-and-Tanged Arrowhead
Early Bronze Age
Flint, L 4.4
Accession no: HCA 036

Throughout the Neolithic period archery was used for both hunting and combat. There is evidence of arrows being used to attack Neolithic settlements and of others found in skeletons. The arrow remained the preferred weapon of the warrior into the Early Bronze Age. A number of burials beneath barrows from this period seem to celebrate the archer. Such graves often contain arrowheads, an archer's wrist-guard and a dagger, all of which were usually finely crafted.

As the Bronze Age progressed, daggers and then spears and swords appear to have replaced bows and arrows as favoured weapons and potent symbols of the warrior. The lozenge-shaped arrowhead shown (HCA 017) has its tip snapped off, a common form of damage when a flint hits its target. Damaged arrowheads were often rejuvenated by additional flaking, which may account for the asymmetry of the barbed and tanged arrowhead (HCA 036).

Archer-Butler Luck Stone

?Irish, 17th century
Rock crystal, gilded copper, H 5 × W 5
Accession no: HCM 152

This charm or amulet, originally owned by
the Butler family of Garnavilla, near Cahir,
County Tipperary, was traditionally
invoked to protect cattle from disease.
Family and neighbours variously dipped it
in drinking water or hung it from a cow's
neck. The crystal ball, which weighs 200g,
is mounted in a gilded copper or bronze
frame with trefoil decoration and a hanging loop. Rock crystal is a colourless
quartz with many inclusions so that no
two pieces are the same. Ancients thought
of it as frozen water and mined it in the
mountains of India. The Greeks attributed
powers both magical and prophetic to it, as
have many civilisations ever since.

Already being worked in the third
millennium before Christ, rock crystal
came into its own in Egypt during the
Fatimid period (969–1171). From the
fourteenth century to the seventeenth,
royalty in Europe were fascinated by it.
Demystification by science was followed in
the nineteenth century by the celebration
of its beauty. Light-penetrating rock crystal
is traditionally symbolic of the Immaculate
Conception, where the Virgin Mary is the
crystal and Jesus Christ the celestial light.

Statuette of a Baboon

Egyptian, ?Ramesside period
(1292–1069 BC)
Limestone, H 19.5 × W 12 × D 12
Accession no: MG 005

This baboon is seen squatting, forearms resting on its knees. A hole drilled into the crown of the head reveals that it was originally provided with a headdress. Other statuettes feature a combination of the sun disc and crescent moon, made of gilded wood. Limestone statues were often brightly painted. The baboon was one of the manifestations of the god Thoth, an Egyptian moon deity, who was also depicted as an ibis-headed man. Thoth was thought to personify divine speech and seen as the god of writing, mathematics, astronomy and healing. Colossal 30-ton baboon statues were set up by Amenhotep III, King of ancient Egypt from 1417–1379 BC, in the temple area at el-Ashmunein in Middle Egypt, one of the principal cult centres of the deity. The associated sacred animal cemeteries at Tuna el-Gebel, Middle Egypt, have yielded mummified baboons in the same pose as this statue. The evidence suggests that many had endured cramped living conditions.

Smaller statuettes, such as this one, may have been dedicated at a temple of Thoth by an official, whose name would have been carved on the base, now lost. Another type of statue depicted officials holding before them a small image of Thoth as a baboon. Through such actions, officials aimed to become closer to the god and ensure an eternal legacy, while visitors to the temple might recite a prayer or place offerings before the statuette.

Polished Stone Axes

?Irish, c.7000–2000 BC
Stone, H 21.3–3.1 × W 9.3–2.8 × D 4.5–1.3
Accession nos: HCA 156; 113; 171; 132; 160;
115; 174

This group of seven stone axes, from a total of 60 in the Hunt Collection, is a small sample of the 20,000 known examples in Ireland. Although generally regarded as artefacts from the Neolithic period, stone axes were in use in Ireland from the Early Mesolithic period through to the Bronze Age. The axes were produced from both common and rare rock sources, with most being flaked or pecked into shape, and finished by grinding and polishing. All axes were made in this way, but the high-quality finish of some completely polished axes raised

them above the everyday woodworking tool to prestigious, ritual and ceremonial use. Many of the Irish axes come from riverbeds and lakes, some of which may be lost items, but it seems certain that others were deliberately deposited votive offerings.

Most stone axes are stray finds, but some have been excavated from Neolithic megalithic tombs and Bronze Age burials, albeit with varying depositional patterns. Depending on their composition and shape, stone axes were also used as adzes, chisels and wedges. This sample includes a large polished gabbro axe, a flaked flint axe, a wide polished jadeite axe, a small polished shale axe, a small polished porcellanite adze/axe, a miniature polished dolerite axe and a polished dolerite adze.

Torso (of Folded-arm Figurine)

Greek, Early Cycladic II / Keros–Seyros
phase, *c.*2700–*c.*2400 BC
White Marble, H 6.1 × W 4.6
Accession no: MG 002

Figurines are the most appealing products
of Cycladic art, and they continue to
inspire painters and sculptors. On this
example the lower legs, neck and head are
missing. The chest is a slight swelling, and
the right arm is placed under the left in the
convention of the 'folded-arm' type. The
fingers are not indicated. On the back,
grooves mark the top of the legs and the
spine. The function of these figurines and
their place in the religious beliefs of the
early Cycladic people has been variously
interpreted. No cult places from the
period have been found, and the context
of most figurines is funerary (although
they are found in only a minority of the
graves in any cemetery). They have also
been discovered in a small number of
settlements.

Opinion is divided as to whether the
figurines were used before burial in the
domestic or public sphere, probably as
cult images, or whether they were always
intended for the grave. That this figure
should have been broken in antiquity
suggests that it may have been damaged
deliberately during a pre-depositional
graveside ritual.

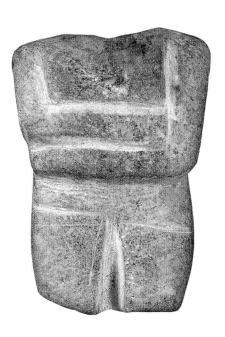

Collared Jar (kandela)

Greek, Early Cycladic I /
Grotta–Pelos phase
(Plastiras group)
*c.*3300–*c.*2400 BC
White marble,
lime encrusted,
H 23.9
Accession no:
MG 001A

The collared jar is the most characteristic of its type from the earliest Early Bronze Age phase of Cycladic civilisation. This vessel has a hemispherical body, a narrow, flat shoulder, a broad, nearly cylindrical neck and a conical foot. Its four vertical lugs, each with a horizontal perforation, are broken at the height of the perforation. This type of vessel, also made in clay, was produced in a wide range of sizes from the miniature to the monumental. It is not clear, however, whether clay or stone was the original medium. Its common name, 'kandela' means lamp, but the shape indicates that it was most probably a container for liquids.

These jars are found in graves, usually wealthy ones, and are occasionally accompanied by marble figurines of the earliest folded-arm type. However, their use may well not have been exclusively funerary. It has been suggested that, since the perforated lugs – which were probably used to suspend the jars from cords so that they could be carried – are often broken, the vases may have been used in the home before being consigned to a grave. Nevertheless, their precise use and possible cultic function remain obscure.

Roman Figurine

Roman, 4th–5th century
Bloodstone, H 8.5 × W 3.5 × D 2.3
Accession no: MG 011

Miniature Portrait Bust

2nd–3rd century
Agate, H 3.1 × W 2 × D 1
Accession no: MG 100

This bloodstone figurine, carved in the round, presents an unarmed nobleman of a certain stature and age, denoted both by the furrowed brow and ungroomed hair, and the beard with ample moustache. This figurine, its feet long gone, may have once been part of a victory trophy. If so, it could have been arranged together with other captive figurines around an image of the emperor or imperial standard. In all likelihood it represents a barbarian noble. The figure wears a crown comprising a simple ring band. The hands are clasped and unbound, poised in an attitude of honourable defeat. He wears long trousers, a long-sleeve tunic, a cloak and an overmantle fastened on the left shoulder with a round brooch. A distinctive fringe to the overmantle suggests a wool weave. The trousers imply a provincial origin. Skilful use of the drill is noted for hair and soft drapery folds. Depictions of barbarians are widespread in Roman art, and comparisons with fourth to fifth century imperial court styles from Constantine to Theodosius provide a stylistic indication of date. Semi-precious cut-stone figurines like this one are now very rare. Comparison should be made with a second century chalcedony captive figurine from the British Museum, London; a fourth-century amethyst Roman empress from the Victoria and Albert Museum, London, and a miniature second to third century agate veiled female portrait bust from the Hunt Museum Collection.

'Line Sinker' with Pater-incised Cross and Small Cross-inscribed Pebble

Irish or Scottish (Stranraer), ?6th–12th
century
Stone, H 7 – H 7
Accession nos: HCA 473; 195

The small artificially shaped stone,
possibly a reused prehistoric macehead of
some sort, is too finely made simply to
have been a net or line sinker for fishing.
On one side there is a small but clearly
incised cross and, on the reverse, four
small circular depressions. These
may have been cut later to represent
(along with the central perforation)
the Five Wounds of Christ.

The small ovoid stone is
decorated with an incised cross
in an oval frame, and a drilled
depression at the junction
of the arms and shaft. Pebbles
of this general form, with a
wide variety of cross forms,
occur in large numbers in Ireland
and in smaller quantities in
Scotland. Various names, including
altar, prayer, curing, priest's, pilgrim's
and turning, have been applied to the
stones. The best known of them are the
famous turning stones on Inishmurray,
County Sligo. A few have been found in
archaeological excavations on High Island,
County Galway, where they occurred in
tenth- to twelfth-century graves.
One from the Aran Islands,
Galway Bay, bears a cross and
the inscription 'A Prayer for
Bran the Pilgrim'. Another from
Kilcorban, County Galway, has
a chi-rho monogram in an oval
frame. Such objects may have
been aids to prayer and mediation
or pilgrims' souvenirs.

Head (Noble Lady)

Roman, 1st century AD
Marble, fine white crystalline,
H 29 × W 17 × D 16.5
Accession no: JB 006

This young woman of simple yet strong, smooth-skinned features tilts her head demurely to the right. Her oval face, set with lightly incised eyebrows and almond-shaped eyes, complements a pronounced thin forehead, a narrow bridged nose, small mouth, pursed lips, pointed chin and sweeping jaw-line. Her wavy hair, in thin ribbed strands, parted in the centre and emphasised by drill work, is drawn across the temples and over the ears, and knotted at the nape of the neck in a bun.

While most of the original polished surface remains a repaired hairline, chipped ears and broken neckline is evident. The original nose is no more, its replacement cracked. Despite the ravages of time, charm, strength and beauty remain. Her demeanour and personality are redolent of the ageless features associated with a Greek goddess, but stylistic and physical characteristics, especially the rendering of the hair and the shape of the eyes, suggest a date during the Julio-Claudian period of the first century.

Axe Mould

?Irish, Early Bronze Age
Stone, H 19 × W 14 × D 7.8
Accession no: HCA 212

This is an early stone mould for casting flat copper or bronze tools in two opposing faces or matrices. The face shown contains a matrix for a flat axe and a smaller axe or chisel-like implement; the opposing one has a matrix for a slightly larger flat axe. Although the edges of the mould have been shaped by pecking, the face with the matrix remains irregular, suggesting that it is unlikely a cover would have been fitted on top. After the axe was cast, it would have been tapered, sharpened and smoothed by hammering and grinding with stone tools. This post-casting work would not only extend the length of the blade but also increase the breadth of the cutting edge. It is difficult, therefore, to determine the exact form of the finished product. As the Bronze Age progressed, more complex two-piece moulds were developed.

Evidence for the earliest copper mining, so far discovered in western Europe, comes from Ross Island in County Kerry. Here the copper ore was extracted by lighting fires and hammering at the rock face of cave-like openings in the limestone. After the ore was extracted it was crushed before smelting in pit furnaces to produce droplets of copper. The copper droplets were then remelted into ingots, which were melted once more and poured into a mould such as the one shown here.

Madonna and Child

French, Burgundy, *c.*1400
Limestone and polychromy, H 84
Accession no: HCM 031

This statue, carved in the round, belongs
to a Gothic type known as 'the beautiful
madonna'. It is characterised by fluidity of
stance, with the left hip cocked, giving a
marked S-shape. The body is given
plasticity by the play of light and dark in
the elaborate draping of a generous
mantle, which is swept up onto the
left hip, before falling to the ground.
A dainty slipper peeps out
underneath. The madonna is
crowned with a pendant veil.
The child, wearing loose clothing,
and whose upper body is missing,
is supported on her left arm, while
with her right hand, she plays
gently with his little toes. Her
expression, as she looks down at his
bare foot, is at once tender and sad.

In the course of conservation,
traces of the original polychromy
were discovered underneath
layers of whitewash that
culminated in modern paint.
This showed how the madonna
had originally been given a blue
gown and a red mantle. Her
face and neck were white,
while there was painted
decoration on the headband
and gold decoration on the face,
hair and veil hem. This gentle,
tender image is characteristic of
carving in Burgundy of the fifteenth
century, with an emphasis on the
emotional involvement of
viewers in the events in the
life of Christ and Mary, his
mother.

Cosmetic Jar

Ancient Egyptian, Middle Kingdom, Second
Intermediate Period (*c.*2040–1550 BC)
Anhydrite, H 4.6 × W 4 × D 4
Accession no: MG 008

This small jar is delicately carved with a
relief representation of two monkeys. The
monkeys are depicted squatting with arms
outstretched to touch the other, a pose
that required the artist to give them
unnaturally long arms. The original source
for this rare stone from which the jar is
made, is unknown, its use almost confined
to the production of small, finely made
cosmetic vessels during the Middle
Kingdom and Second Intermediate
Period. Other such types include figures
of monkeys holding cosmetic jars and
containers in the form of trussed ducks.
Monkeys appear on stelae and tomb
reliefs of the same period, and may even
have been kept as pets by the élite. Such
artefacts may have formed part of their
burial goods. Objects found in tombs
were often specifically manufactured for
that purpose.

An intact burial of the late seventeenth
dynasty at Thebes (*c.*1600 BC), found by
Flinders Petrie in 1909, provides an
example of the type of context in which
such bowls were used. Set into a shallow
trench, protected by natural boulders, was
the coffin of a woman, her burial goods
arranged around her. Alongside much
pottery, some of it slung in nets attached to
a long pole, the burial contained basketry,
a wooden headrest, food offerings and
three wooden chairs. A single vessel
carved from anhydrite was included,
featuring four monkeys on the exterior.

Two Daggers

Scandinavian, Late
Neolithic/Early Bronze Age
Flint, L 17.7; 25.3
Accession nos: MG 139/087;
HCA 066

Daggers became important symbols of power in the Bronze Age. Many of them have been found accompanying male graves under barrows. Metal daggers were used in areas where metal ores were accessible, but in regions without metal resources, such as Scandinavia, flint was used. Some of the later flint daggers, such as those shown here, are imitations of metal daggers.

These two daggers were made with exceptional skill, using a flint-knapping method known as pressure-flaking.

With this technique, flakes are removed by applying pressure with the tip of an antler or some other soft instrument rather than being struck off by a hard blow from a hammer-stone. On HCA 066, the line of raised zigzag pattern down the middle of the handle and along its edges may be an imitation of stitching on a leather-covered handle. The blade has also been partially polished to give it a smoother appearance.

Olmec Man

Mexican, c.900–400 BC
Jade or serpentine, H 34 × W 13 × D 9.5
Accession no: L 003

This sculpture has its origins in the Olmec civilisation, the most ancient in Mesoamerica. The Olmec, from the Gulf Coast of Mexico, are distinguished from their predecessors by a social structure that highlighted contrasts in status and wealth. It has been suggested they laid the foundations for later cultures, such as the Mayan. Our understanding of the Olmec is based on their hallmark art style. This was produced on a monumental scale, such as colossal heads of basalt, and on a small scale, such as finely polished carved-stone articles.

Carvings left by Olmec masons suggest a society based on centralised political and religious authority. The central theme is the 'were-jaguar', a concept unifying feline and sexless human characteristics. Distinctive features include many of those exhibited in this statue, such as a snarling mouth and prominent thick upper lip, toothless gums, bent legs, a flat nose and a proportionally large and bald head with cranial deformations. Its provenance is unknown, but this figure is similar to those found in an elaborate burial at the formative site, La Venta. Among its offerings was a cache with nearly identical jade and serpentine figurines, a type known only to La Venta. This example differs in its apparent mutilation of the arms and head, a practice commonly related to the abandonment of Olmec sites.

Sheela-na-gig Carving

Irish, 15th century
Limestone, H 48 × W 33
Accession no: HCM 033

Sheela-na-gigs are to be seen on some eleventh- and twelfth-century churches in France and Britain, but the greatest number occurs in Ireland, on both church and secular structures dating from the twelfth century to the sixteenth. Their original meaning and function is uncertain. Current theories include a warning against the sin of lust, a fertility symbol, a guardian or protector, a depiction of a Celtic goddess.

This carving was brought to the attention of John Hunt by workmen who found it while repairing a stone bridge at Lough Gur, County Limerick, in 1946. The head and parts of the legs are missing, but the torso and arms are in good condition. Unusually for a sheela-na-gig, the breasts and navel are well defined, and the vulva, although remarkable, is not as grotesquely exaggerated as on similar figures. The figure may be more naturalistic and correct than the majority of such carvings: not so unskilled nor as much of a caricature. Often erroneously described as exhibitionist figures because of their overt sexual display, sheela-na-gigs share several characteristics that differentiate them from true exhibitionists. They are solitary, female and anatomically distorted, and their placement is liminal. Other exhibitionists, however, are often part of figure groups, may be male or female, are anatomically correct and seldom liminal.

Relief Carving of St James of Compostela

Spanish, *c.*1500
Jet, H 11 × W 6.5 × D 1.7
Accession no: MG 044

During the Middle Ages pilgrims travelled
in great numbers to the shrine of St James
at Santiago de Compostela in Spain, and a
variety of religious souvenirs was made to
cater for them. The more affluent pilgrim
might have been able to afford *azabaches*
carved in jet. These were manufactured on
such a large scale throughout the fifteenth
and sixteenth centuries that a guild of
azabacheros was established at Compostela
in 1443.

    Jet is hard and brittle, making it a
difficult material to carve, but once the
surfaces are polished the effects can be
stunning. Although the plaque in the
Museum has suffered damage over the
years, it displays many typical features:
St James has an impressive beard and
stands barefooted, with a kneeling
pilgrim or disciple to one side. The saint
clasps a staff in his right hand, from
which hangs a purse and rosary beads.
There is a hint of a second purse, hanging
from his belt, but no sign of the book
normally depicted in his left hand. Far
more characteristic is the wide-brimmed
hat, ornamented with a scallop shell, the
latter being the celebrated emblem of the
shrine of St James. Although it is not
known where this *azabache* was
found, some details are reproduced in
Irish stone carvings of the time,
suggesting that souvenirs of this
type were brought back by Irish
pilgrims.

Tazza

German, 17th century
Lapis lazuli, silver gilt,
H 14 × W 18 × D 18
Accession no: CG 020

The Italian *tazza* comes from the Arabic *tassah*, meaning cup. This is a luxurious example of *pietra dura*, the decorative use of hardstones. This art, which had its roots in Classical antiquity and Byzantium, reached its high point in sixteenth-century Milan and Florence under Medici sponsorship. This technique was mostly used for inlaid wall panels for interiors, but dwindling Medici fortunes caused a shift to more portable, saleable items such as tabletops, vases and cups. Artists also relocated to the European kingdoms, where there was a fashion for beautiful objects, of rare and exotic materials, which were displayed in treasuries.

This cup and base, which were shaped on a lathe, are of lapis lazuli, a blue-grey and black mottled stone mainly of silica and alumina, which is found in Siberia, Turkey, China and Afghanistan. The stem and mounts on the rim and base are of silver gilt. The rim has a beaded motif, and the centrepiece is a rosette of flowers and leaves. The stem is cast and features a repeated motif of alternating rams' and lions' heads, with pendant sprays and swags, between rings, and an upright palmette motif on its base. The base has a cut-card rim. Recessed under the base is a plate with four ovoid cut-outs, each framed in a cartouche, four panels of fruit and a central rosette, all chased.

Carved Stone Ceremonial Ball

?Scottish, Late Neolithic
Stone, Diam. 6.4
Accession no: HCA 207

The dull appearance of this ball belies the sophistication of the pattern of the bosses on the surface, carved by a craftsman with an understanding of the concept of trigonometry and its relationship to spherical shapes. The carving indicates an appreciation of spherical co-ordinates and perhaps reflects a knowledge of celestial movements shown in the layout of many prehistoric sites such as Newgrange. The four large bosses, equidistant from each other and representing a spherical version of the tetrahedron, are surrounded by circles of nine smaller bosses, which merge, giving a total of 24 small bosses set out in a definite pattern. Three of the large bosses have grooved incisions, which do not appear to represent any recognisable pattern, such as the spiral, concentric circle or geometric design, found on other similar objects.

Nearly all of the 400 examples recorded come from Scotland, and most are approximately 7 cm in diameter with a wide variety of design and decoration. Most of the balls are stray finds, but those found in the Neolithic houses at Scara Brae in the Orkneys, when combined with the similarity of some of the decoration to that found in passage tombs, suggest a late Neolithic date and possible continued use in the Bronze Age. Despite much discussion,their purpose remains unclear, but it seems certain that they were prestige items and probably symbols of power with ceremonial functions.

INDEX

Page numbers in *italics* include
references to illustrations.

agate miniature portrait bust *161*
albarello *41*
Altar Cross with Crucified Christ *97*
altarpiece *27*
amulet *156*
Anglo-Norman crosier *90*
anhydrite jar *166*
annunciation canopy or baldachin
    151
Antrim Cross, The *119*
Apollo, figure of *140*
Apulian *lebes gamikos* *47*
aquamanile *98*
Arabic:
    influence *51*; cylindrical casket *83*
Archer-Butler Luck Stone *156*
Arita *71, 72, 74*
armlet *122*
Armstrong, Robert William *39*
arrowheads *155*
Astor, Lord *82*
Augsburg, Germany *109, 140*
Avignon *141*
axe *12*
    bronze and copper *99*;
    mould *164*; polished stone *158*

baboon, statuette of *157*
baldachin *151*
ball, ceremonial *172*
Ball Collection, St Alban's *101*
ball-type brooch *100*
Ballylongford Cross *137*
Ballyscullion Cauldron *126, 130*
Balthasar, statue of *152*
baluster jug:
    earthenware *56*; stoneware *58*
Baroque *35*
barrel *60*
Bavarian figures *46*
Bayerisches Nationalmuseum,
    Munich *98*
beaked flagon *101*
beakers *92*
Beaufort, Turenne and Comminges
    Tapestry Fragment *141*
Beckwith, John *84*
bell:
    bronze *104*; Gerfalcon *145*
Belleek pottery *39*
Benin ornament *93*
Berlin ironwork tiara and necklace
    120
Beverley Crozier, The *90*
bloodstone figurine *161*
Bohemia *92, 101*
bone, hawk's call or whistle *145*,
    carving *79*
Böttger, Johannes *68*
bourdaloue *44*
Bourke KCB, General Sir Richard
    54

bowl *108, 109*
    clay food vessel *43*; delftware *62*;
    Imari ware *72*; silver-gilt
    mounted *52*; stone-paste *51*
box *106*
bracelet *122*
brass aquamanile *98*
brass carvings *93*
Britain *36, 93, 122*,
    Roman *136*
British Museum, London *9, 84, 86,*
    124, 150, 161
Brodrick, Alan and Thomas *111*
Bromley, William *39*
bronze *34, 89, 93, 124*
    altar cross *97*; armlet and torque
    122; axe heads *99*; bell *104*; bucket
    130; cauldron *126*; chasse *102, 116*;
    cross *119*; crucifix *94–96*;
    dodecahedron *134*; escutcheon
    disc *108*; figure of a man *105*;
    figure of a horse *127*; figure of
    Horus *110*; flagon *101*;
    hand warmer *129*; pendants or
    Y-shaped pieces *125*; shield *128*;
    spearheads *103*; tools *164*;
    wine strainer *133*
Bronze Age *105, 160*
    arrowheads *155*; axe heads *99, 158*;
    axe mould *164*; cauldron *126*;
    ceremonial balls *172*; crannóg *17*;
    daggers *167*; funerary pottery *43*;
    gold torque *124*; shield *128*;
    spearheads *103*
brooch *105*
    copper alloy *135, 136*; Pegasus *138*;
    silver ball-type *100*
bucket *101, 128, 130*
Bunratty Castle, Co. Clare *15–16*
Burrell Collection *141*
Burrell, Sir William *9*
bust *161*
Bustelli, Franz Anton *46*

Caherguillemore, Co. Limerick *15*
candelabrum *39*
Cannock Tait & Co. decanter *91*
canopy *151*
Canosa, Italy *92*
Cape Castle Bucket, The *130*
card tray *123*
carved stone ceremonial ball *172*
carving:
    bone *79*; brass *93*; Christ the
    Good Shepherd *78*; Isis Suckling
    Horus *79*; John the Evangelist *88*;
    Man on Horseback *146*;
    sheela-na-gig *169*; St James of
    Compostela *170*; St Thomas à
    Becket *89*; Flight into Egypt, the
    144
Cashel Bell *104*
Cashel Pyx, The *106*
casket:
    bronze *102*; ivory *83*
cauldron *126, 128, 130*
Caulfield, James, Viscount
    Charlemont *38*

Celtic:
    figures *105*; flagon *101*;
    goddess *169*; Iron Age *122, 125*;
    metalwork *108*
ceramics *38–75, 154*
ceremonial ball *172*
chalice *109, 112, 131*
Chantilly *44*
Charlemont dinner service plates
    38
Charles II, King *111, 115*
charm *156*
chasse *102, 116*
Chinese:
    bourdaloue *44*; dinner service
    plates *38*; jar and cover *70*;
    mounted bowl *52*;
    porcelain *38, 52, 61, 63, 64, 67,*
    68, 69, 70, 71, 73, 75;
    pug dogs *73*; sweetmeat dish *69*;
    wine ewer *75*
Christ Church Cathedral, Dublin
    142
Christ the Good Shepherd, carving
    of *78*
Church of Ireland plate *112*
clay:
    food vessels *43*; *lebes gamikos* *47*;
    lekythos *48*; plastic vessel *50*
Clonroad More, Co. Clare *15*
coin, Syracuse *9, 107*
collared jar *160*
Cologne *59, 83, 152*
comb *82*
communion cup *112*
Connolly, Sybil *154*
copper *57*
    amulet *156*; axe head *99*; handpin
    136; processional cross *137*;
    ringed pins *118*; tools *164*;
    zoomorphic penannular
    brooch *135*
coral ring *81*
cosmetic jar *166*
County Antrim *103, 126, 128, 130,*
    135
County Down *99, 104*
County Limerick *9, 15, 37, 54, 99,*
    100, 125
Craggaunowen Castle, Co. Clare *15,*
    16–17, 18
crannóg *17*
creamware *66*
crosier *90*
cross *96*
    bronze *97, 119*; gilt copper alloy
    137; gold *18, 117*; Gyldensteen *84*;
    lead penal *132*; 'line sinker' *162*;
    pendant *114*; rosary *139*
crucifix:
    bronze *94–96*; wood *142*
Cycladic era:
    collared jar (kandela) *160*;
    sculpture *9, 159*
cylindrical casket *83*

Daddi, Bernardo *28*
daggers *43, 103, 155, 167*

Danish Bronze Age 105
Daphne, Greece 88
da Venezia, Domenico 42
da Vinci, Leonardo 18, 127
decanter 91
decorative hand warmer 129
dekadrachma of Syracuse 107
Delamain pottery plate 61
delftware 67
    barrel 60; *bourdaloue* 44;
    hors-d'oeuvre set 63; plate 61, 64;
    punchbowl 62; water bottle and
    wash-basin 65
devotional diptych panel 87
dinner service plates 38
disc 108
dish:
    ceramic 40; porcelain 54, 59
dodecahedron 134
Doran, Professor Patrick 18
Downshire Pottery 66
Dresden 53, 68, 71, 73
drinking cup 50
drinking horn 76
drinking vessels 153
drug jar 41, 42
Drumleck, Co. Dublin 11-15, 13
Dublin 10, 25, 35, 91, 112, 122, 154
    assay office 121; Cathedral 142;
    delftware 60–64; tapestries 149;
    Viking 118
Dunlevy, Mairead 7
Dutch:
    Dogs 73; earthenware tankard 67;
    painting 27, 30; stoneware 59;
    vases 86

earthenware 59
    drug jar 41, 42; jug 56; pharmacy
    jar 45; pilgrim flask 49; tankard
    67; watering pot 57
Egypt 41, 144
Egyptian:
    bone carving 79; cosmetic jar 166;
    figures 9, 110, 150, 157; rock
    crystal 156
Elizabeth Forth Chalice 131
England 52, 58, 59, 60, 66
English:
    baluster jug 56; carving 89; cross
    84; crucifix 95, 96; delftware 60,
    64, 65, 67; drawing 36;
    escutcheon disc 108; flagons 101;
    hand warmer 129; painting 32, 33,
    35; pearlware 66; pomander 115;
    porcelain 63, 64; processional
    cross 136; Reformation 112;
    reliquary cross 114, 117;
    stained-glass 77; torque 124;
    water bottle and wash-basin 65;
    watering pot 57
escutcheon disc 108
Etruscan:
    beaked flagon 101; jewellery 81
evening gown 154
ewer 75

Fagan, Robert 19, 33

faience pilgrim flask 49
falconry paraphernalia 145
figures:
    bronze 110, 105; ivory 78;
    porcelain 46, 74; wooden 140, 144,
    146, 147
figurines 159, 161
five-decade rosary 139
flagon 101
flask 49
flat axes 99, 164
Flemish painting 30
Flight into Egypt, carving of the 144
flint:
    arrowheads 155; axe 158;
    daggers 167
Florence, Italy 28, 29, 45, 86, 127,
    171
Folk Park, Bunratty Castle 15–17
food vessels 43
Frechen mug 59
French:
    bourdaloue 44; canopy or
    baldachin 151; carving 144;
    crucifix 142; chasse 102, 116;
    earthenware 56; devotional panel
    87; Iron Age 122; ivory comb 82;
    painting 24, 26, 29; pilgrim flask
    49; sheela-na-gigs 169; statue 165;
    tapestry fragment 141
Friends of the Hunt Museum 8, 19
Froment, Nicolas 29
funerary pottery 43

Gallimore, William Wood 39
Galway 131, 162
Galway Chalice 131
Galway Rosaries 139
Galway Sword 131
Gauguin, Paul 19, 24, 31
Georgian Ireland 61
German:
    altarpiece 27; aquamanile 98;
    baluster jug 58; canopy or
    baldachin 151; drinking horn 76;
    earthenware 67; Frechen mug 59;
    liturgical 'heel' spoon 108;
    Meissen porcelain 53–55, 58;
    plaque 84; carving 88; tazza 171;
    painting 27, 30; Pietà 53; serving
    dish 54; snuff-box 55; stoneware
    59, 67; tureens 68; wooden
    figures 140, 143, 152, 147, 148;
    Zwishengoldglas beakers 92
Germany 9, 59, 83, 86, 97, 134
Giacometti, Alberto 9, 34
Gibney, Arthur 18
glass:
    decanter 91; jug 86; stained 77;
    Zwishengoldglas beakers 92
Goble, Robert 111
gold:
    brooch 138; decoration 165;
    foil 92; love pair pendant 80;
    pomander 115; reliquary cross 114,
    117; ring 81; torque 124
Golden Vale 16
Gort, Lord 15

Goss, William Henry 39
Gothic style 27, 76, 82, 87, 94, 148,
    151; neo-Gothic design 120;
    revival 96; statue 165
gown, evening 154
Granta Fen torque 124
Gray, William 130
Greek:
    Apulian *lebes gamikos* 47; carving
    79; collared jar (kandela) 160;
    dekadrachma coin 9, 107; *lekythos*
    48; plastic vessel 50; rock crystal
    156; stone figurine 159; wooden
    statue 150
Gyldensteen, Count Bernstorff 84
Gyldensteen Cross 84

Hallstatt period 105
Hals, Frans 149
handpin 136
hand warmer 129
hanging bowl escutcheon disc 108
hawk's call or whistle 145
hawk's hood 145
hawk's rings 145
head (noble lady) 163
Hearst Foundation 9
'heel' spoon, silver 109
Heintze, Johann George 55
Herculaneum 80, 133
Herold, J.G. 55
Holbein the Younger, Hans 52
hood, hawk's 145
horn 76
hors-d'oeuvre set 63
horse aquamanile 98
Horus 78, 110
Hunt, Gertrude 7, 9–15, 12, 17, 18,
    19
Hunt, John 7, 9–17, 12, 19, 31, 75,
    82, 84, 101, 131, 150, 169
Hunt, John and Trudy 7, 11, 12, 18
Hunt Museum, formation of 7–19
Hunt Museums Trust 18, 19

illumination 90, 116
Imari ware bowl and cover 72
Impressionism 26, 31
Indo-Portuguese figure 78
Ireland 7, 17, 18, 58, 98, 113
    medieval 16, 98, 137
Irish:
    amulet 156; axe mould 164; axes
    99, 158; barrel 60; bell 104; brooch
    100, 135; bucket 130; candelabrum
    39; cauldron 126; chalice 131;
    communion cup 112; craftsmen
    136; cross 119; crucifix 95, 142;
    decanter 91; delftware 60–64;
    dinner services 38; escutcheon
    disc 108; evening gown 154;
    funerary pottery 43; horn 76;
    hors-d'oeuvre set 63; 'line sinker'
    and pebble 162; mace 111;
    maquette 154; metalwork 100,
    111, 113, 130, 135; methers 153;
    neck-rings 113; painting 25, 31, 33,
    35, 37; pap boat feeding vessel 121;

penal cross *132*; pendants or
Y-shaped pieces *125*; pilgrims
170; plate *61, 64, 66*; processional
crosses *137*; punchbowl *62*; pyx
106; ringed pins *118*; rosary *139*;
salver or card tray *123*; sheela-na-
gig *169*; shield *128*; spearheads
103; tapestries *149*; torques *122,
124*; Viking settlements *118*;
zoomorphic penannular brooch
135
Iron Age, *135*
armlet and torque *122*; pendants
or Y-shaped pieces *125*
ironwork tiara and necklace *120*
Isis Suckling Horus, carving of *78*
Islamic influence *41, 51, 83*
Italian:
altar cross *97*; ceramics *40*; coral
ring *81*; drug jar *41, 42*; horse
figure *127*; jug *86*; Maiolica *41, 42,
45*; painting *28*; pharmacy jar *42*
ivory:
Benin ornament *93*; carving *88,
89*; comb *82*; cross *84*; cylindrical
casket *83*; devotional diptych
panel *87*; figure *78*; love pair
pendant *80*; plaque *85*

jade sculpture *168*
Japanese:
bourdaloue 44; bowl and cover *72*;
figures *74*; porcelain *68, 69, 71,
72, 74*; Rouleau vases *71*
jars:
earthenware *41, 42, 45, 49*; marble
160; porcelain *70*; stone *166*
Jeannerat collection, London *127*
jet relief carving *170*
jewellery:
brooch *138*; coral ring *81*; love pair
pendant *80*; reliquary cross *114,
117*; tiara and necklace *120*
John the Evangelist *88, 148*
Johns, Joseph *121, 123*
jug *50, 57*
baluster *56, 58*; glass *86*; Malling
67; Raeren *76*
Julia and Ottavio figures *46*

kandela *160*
Kändler, Johann Joachim *53, 73*
Kavanagh Charter horn *76*
ko-sometsuke 69
knobbed bronze armlet and
cast-bronze torque *122*
Kraak porcelain *52*

lapis lazuli tazza *171*
lead inlay *93*
lead penal cross *132*
leather falconry paraphernalia *145*
lebes gamikos 47
lekythos 48, 50
Leoni, Pompeo *127*
leopard's head ornament *93*
Limerick *7, 9, 18, 25, 35, 91, 121,
123*

Limerick Corporation *19*
Limerick Custom House *7, 16, 17,
19*
limestone:
sheela-na-gig *169*; statue *165*;
statuette *157*
limewood figures *140, 142, 147, 152*
Limoges *102, 116*
linen evening gown and maquette
154
'line sinker' and pebble *162*
liturgical 'heel' spoon *109*
Londesborough, Lord *108, 124*
London *24, 31, 32, 33, 36, 44, 56*
Lough Derg, Co. Mayo *132*
Lough Gur, Co. Limerick *10, 11, 15,
16, 169*
love pair pendant *80*
Lowry, Strickland *35*
Luther, Martin *147*
Lutheran art *30*

mace *111*
Madonna, Romanesque *143*
Madonna and Child *165*
Maggi, Giovanni *86*
Maiolica:
drug jar *41, 42*; pharmacy jar *45*
Malling jugs *67*
Man on Horseback, Carving of a *146*
maquette *154*
marble:
collared jar (kandela) *160*;
head *163*
Mary, Queen of Scots, Cross *18, 117*
Medici *171*
medieval:
armour *15*; altarpiece *27*; art *9, 11*;
chasse *116*; churches *142*;
Ireland *17, 98, 137*; painting *27*;
table *12*; weapons *111*
Meissen *44, 61, 73*
Pietà *53*; serving dish *54*;
snuff-box *55*; tureens *68*
memento mori 115
Mesolithic period *158*
metal objects *94–139*
methers *153*
Metropolitan Museum of Art, New
York *9, 52, 127, 141, 146*
Middle Ages *41, 116, 152, 170*
plaques *85*; hand warmers *129*
Midleton Mace *111*
miniature portrait bust *161*
Ming dynasty *52, 69, 70, 75*
Emperor Wan Li *52*
mokozuke 69
Mosan:
crucifix *94*; plaque *84*
mug, Frechen *59*
Mulvany, John George *37*
Museo Civico, Turin *86*
Museum of Fine Arts,
Budapest *127*

Naples *81, 86*
Napoleon *120*
National Museum of Ireland *76, 111*
necklace *120*
neck-ring *113*
Neo-classical motifs *120*
Neo-Gothic design *120*
Neolithic:
axes *99, 158*; arrowheads *155*;
ceremonial ball *172*; daggers *167*;
Europe *7*; house *12, 15*
Netherlands *59, 67, 71, 73*
Netherlandish School *29*
Nevers pottery *49*
noble lady sculpture *163*
Nuremberg *98*
Nymphenburg pottery *46*

oak carving *146*
O'Conor, Roderic *18, 31*
oenochoë 101
Office of Public Works *7, 19*
O'Kelly, Professor *15*
Olmec Man *168*

Packer, Michael *144*
painting *12, 23–37, 89*
palstave *99*
panel, devotional diptych *87*
pap boat feeding vessel *121*
Paris *24, 33, 87, 120*
Pawlet, Richard *149*
pearlware plate *66*
pearwood figure *148*
pebble, inscribed *162*
Peeckelhaering 149
Pegasus brooch *138*
penal cross, lead *132*
pendant *138*
bronze *108*; ivory and jewels *80*;
reliquary cross *114*; Y-shaped
pieces *125*
Persia *41, 45, 51, 152*
pharmacy jar *45*
Picasso, Pablo *19, 23, 32*
Pietà *53*
pilgrim flask *49*
pins *118, 136*
Pitt-Rivers, General Augustus *93,
124*
Pitt-Rivers Museum *126, 128, 130*
plaque with nativity scenes *85*
plastic vessel *50*
plates:
Delamain pottery *61*; delftware
64; pearlware *66*; porcelain *38*
polished stone axes *158*
polychromed stone *165*
polychromed wooden figures *140,
142, 143, 144, 146, 147, 152*
Polynesian culture *24*
pomander *115*
Pompeii *80, 133*
porcelain
bowl and cover *72*; dinner
service plates *38*; dish *69*; jar and
cover *70*; figures *74*; mounted
bowl *52*; Pietà *53*; pug dogs *73*;

Rouleau vases 71; serving dish 54; snuff-box 55; sweetmeat dish 69; tureens 68; wine ewer 75
Portuguese influence 78
post-Impressionism 24, 31
processional cross 137
Proost, Ludovicus 30
Prussian ironwork tiara and necklace 120
pug dogs 73
'Pugin' crucifix, The 95, 96
punchbowl 63
puppy and kitten figures 74
pyx 105

Qing dynasty 70, 73, 75
Queen Anne design 111

Raeren jugs 76
'Rainer' Crucifix, The 94
Ramesside period 157
Raqqan-style bowl 51
rearing horse 19, 127
'Red Abbey' Crucifix, The 95
Reformation 30, 112, 142
relief carving of St James of Compostela 170
reliquary cross 114, 117
reliquary chasse 116
Renaissance 27, 35
  jugs 58, 86
Renoir, Pierre Auguste 18, 26
Reyley, Daniel 149
Rhineland 101
Rijksmuseum, Amsterdam 141
ring 138
  coral 81; hawk's 145
ringed pins 118
ringfort 17
Robinson, T.W.U. 126, 128, 130
rock crystal charm 156
Romanesque:
  chasse 116; Christ Crucified 142; crucifixes 94–97; Enthroned Madonna 143; plaque 85
Roman:
  Britain 136; catacombs 152; Empire 134; figurine 161; glass 92; head 163; influence 79, 87, 101, 135; wine strainer 133
rosary 139
Rothschild Collection 86
Rouen style 56
Rouleau vases 71
Royal Irish Academy 38
Ryan, Dr Tony 7, 18

salver 123
Scandinavian:
  brooches 100; crucifix 95; daggers 167; drinking horn 76; neck-rings 113
Schinkel, Karl Friedrich 120
Schnulgen, Christian 58
Schnütgen-Museum, Cologne 83
Scottish:
  aquamaniles 98; ceremonial ball 172; food vessels 43; influence 39;

'line sinker' and pebble 162; methers 153; neck-rings 113; pearlware 66; torques 122
sculpture 12, 168
serpentine sculpture 168
serving dish 54
Severin, Tim 17
sheela-na-gig carving 169
shield, bronze 128
Shou Fu 52
Siculo-Arabic cylindrical casket 83
Siegburg baluster jug 58
silver 72
  ball-type brooch 100; chalice 131; communion cup 112; dekadrachma 107; falconry paraphernalia 145; 'heel' spoon 109; mace 111; neck-ring 113; pap boat feeding vessel 121; pyx 106; rosary 139; salver or card tray 123
silver-gilt:
  bowl 52; horn mounts 76; jug mounts 58, 59; tazza 171
skull 115
snuff-box 55
socketed axes 99
Sotheby's 9, 11, 84
Spanish
  ceramic dish 40; earthenware 41; figure 148; painting 23; relief carving 170; reliquary cross 114, 117; rosaries 139; vases 86; spearheads 103
spoon 109
Stacpoole, George 7–8
stained-glass panel 77
'Stag's Head' candelabrum 39
statues 143, 150, 152, 153, 165
statuette of a baboon 157
stone objects 155–172
  arrowheads 155; axes 99, 158; amulet 156; axe mould 164; ceremonial ball 172; cosmetic jar 166; daggers 167; figurines 159, 161; 'line sinker' and pebble 162; sculpture 163, 168; sheela-na-gig 169; statue 165; statuette 157
Stone Age 9
stone-paste bowl 51
stoneware 65, 67
  baluster jug 58; Frechen mug 59
St Anne with the Christ Child and Virgin Mary 147
St Brendan boat 17
St James of Compostela, relief carving of 170
St John of Beverley 90
St John the Evangelist 88, 148
strainer 133
St Thomas à Becket 89, 114
sweetmeat dish 69
Swiss sketch 34
Syracuse, dekadrachma coin 9, 107
Syrian Raqqan-style bowl 51

tankard:
  Dutch 67; Frechen mug 59

tapestry 12, 89, 141, 149
tazza 171
Tène period, La 105
  metalwork 108; armlet and torque 122
tiara 120
torque:
  bronze 122; gold 124
Torso (of a folded-arm figurine) 159
tray, silver 123
Triptych: Painted Epitaph 30
Tudor 57, 137
Tureens 68, 72
Tymbos workshop 48
Tyson jar 70

Uffizi, Florence 29, 86
United States of America 62, 66
University of Limerick (formally National Institution for Higher Education) 7, 18-19
urinal 44

van der Weyden, Rogier 29
van Hoogstraten, Samuel 35
vases 86
  clay food vessel 43; lekythos 48, 50; plastic vessel 50; Rouleau 71
Venice drug jars 41, 42
vessels 43, 47, 48, 50, 121
Veste Coburg collection 86
Victoria and Albert Museum, London 137, 161
Viking 100, 119, sculptures 105; ringed pins 118, neck-ring 113
Voak, Jonathan 7

Wade and Partners, Robin 19
Walsh, Dr Edward 7, 19
wash-basin 65
watering pot 57
water bottle 65
wedding vessel 47
Wedgwood 44
whistle 145
Wilder, Samuel 112
Wilson, Peter 9
wine:
  barrel 60; ewer 75; strainer 133
Winston, Charles 77
wooden:
  canopy or baldachin 151; figures 105, 140, 142, 143, 144, 146, 147, 148, 150, 152; hawk's call or whistle 145; methers 153
wool:
  garments 136; hawk's hood 145; tapestry fragment 141; tapestries 149
Wormald, Professor Francis 90

Yeats, Jack B. 25
Y-shaped pieces 125

zoomorphic penannular brooch 135, 136
Zwishengoldglas beakers 92